PROPERTY OF
TED D. MARSZALEK
MARCH 1, 1996

WHAT REVIEWERS SAY ABOUT
MASTERING INTERNETWORKING

"[The] **highly readable style** was enjoyable and the insights informative...Keep up the good work of addressing an often misunderstood arena of communications technology."
—Harrell Van Norman, consultant/author in network performance and optimization

"An **exceptionally good** study guide that will enable the earnest student to firmly grasp the complexities of LAN internetworking. Upon completion of this series, the network manager should be able to cut through vendor hoopla and cull the most salient information necessary to successfully build a corporate internetwork."
—Maureen Molloy, Network World

"...**communicates concepts extremely well**. Takes a **real-world,** hands-on approach." **Rated A** (= excellent)
—Computer Book Review

"**Invaluable**! A sure-fire winner with other working network managers, here and elsewhere in Europe."
—E. C., Network Manager, Dublin Ireland

"I can understand internetworking now! Thank you for producing something **readable**, that doesn't talk down to me. For someone in voice comm, making the transition to data comm manager has been hard…**this makes it easy**."

  —InternationalTelecom Manager, SFSU
  Extension participant

"**Best of the lot**—and I've read a lot!…eminently readable and the material is accurate, **especially good in bridging and routing**…Can't wait to see Advanced Internetworking"

  —Sadie Lewis, voice/data network consultant

"**Well-done**, almost effortless learning, written simply, light of jargon, with **terms clearly defined** as they come up. The information is all there, most often graphically depicted. It is also **instructionally sound**—it starts with review of the basics and gradually builds new information on what has already been clearly presented."

  —Rita Lewis, Instructional Designer

"Now there's a middle ground [between live training and consultants]: a self learning guide that **allows net managers to go at their own pace** and ask questions about their networks along the way.… The exams at the end of each chapter take some unusual forms, from internetwork design projects to crossword puzzles."

  —Data Communications Magazine

Mastering
Advanced Internetworking

Self-Paced Learning Series

V. C. Marney-Petix

Numidia Press
Fremont, CA 94536

Mastering Advanced Internetworking
Self-Paced Learning Series

©1993 Victoria C. Marney-Petix

All rights reserved. No part of this book may be reproduced in any way, or by any means, electronic or mechanical, or by any information storage and retrieval system without permission in writing from the publisher.

Printed in the United States of America.

All trademarks are registered to their respective owners. Casual use of company names and products in these pages does not imply that these trademarks are in the public domain.

Editorial & Marketing Team: Gail Hillocks, Becky Harris and Sherri Magdziak
Design, Layout & Illustration Team: Dawn Dombrow and Lisa Hamm

Library of Congress Cataloging-In-Publication Data

Marney-Petix, V.C. (Victoria C.)
    Mastering Advanced Internetworking / V.C. Marney-Petix.
        p. cm. - - (Self-paced learning series)
    Includes bibliographical references and index.
    ISBN 1-880548-25-9 : $24.95
    1. Computer networks. 2. Local area networks (Computer networks)
    3. Wide area networks (Computer networks) I. Title   II. Series.
TK5105.5.M3594   1993
004.6 - - dc20   93-173
                                                      CIP

Table of Contents

Preface ix

Acknowledgments xi

Chapter 0 – Internetworking Review
Internetworking – The Puzzle 6

Chapter 1 – Architectures Review
Reviewing The OSI Model 10
Network Infrastructures 12
SNA: New and Old 14
XNS, Novell and DECnet 16
The Internet 18
Reviewing Internet Devices 20

Chapter 2 – Advanced Bridging
Kinds of Bridges 24
Transparent Bridges 26
Let's Build a Spanning Tree 28
SR, SRT and SR-TB Bridging 30
Source Route Bridging Gotchas 32
Bridge Performance Issues 34
Linking Architectures: Tunnelling/Passthrough 36
Switching Bridges 38
Future of Bridging 40

Chapter 3 – Advanced Routing
Modern Routing Technology 46
Problems With Distance Vectors 48
Link State Routing 50
Link State Routing In Detail 52
Subnetting 54
Inter-Domain Routing 56
OSI and IP Addressing 58

Multiple Routing Protocols 60
Ships in the Night vs. Integrated Routing 62
Routing Unroutable Traffic 64
Wide-Area Routing 66
The Future of Routing 68

Chapter 4 – Network Operating Systems & Middleware

Servers, Network Operating Systems and Middleware 76
Rise of Client/Server Computing 78
NOS Market Survey 80
NetWare 82
VINES 84
LAN Manager 86
LAN Server and Device OSs 88
Choosing A NOS 90
Middleware 92
The Evolution of NOSs and Middleware 94

Chapter 5 – MAN and WAN Internetworking

Introducing MANs 100
MAN and WAN Technologies 102
DQDB Technology 104
SMDS Service Interfaces 106
The SMDS and SONET Technology 108
Packet, Circuit and Cell Switching 110
The Broadband ISDN Model 112
Planning An ATM Strategy 114
Frame Relay – Part 2 116
Public or Private Network 118
Integrating MAN/WAN Technologies 120
Managing an Integrated MAN/WAN 122
A Tale of Two Network Managers 124
Looking to the Future 126

Chapter 6 – Backbones & Multi-Protocol Internets

Why Multi-Protocol? 132
Introducing Backbones 134
Should You Collapse Your Backbone? 136
Horrible Case #1: The Campus With Too Many Repeaters . 138
The Evolution of SNA 140
Eliminating Parallel Networks 142
Working With APPN 144
TCP/IP and OSI 146
The Skinny Stack Proposal 148
DEC Advantage Networks 150
Multiple Towers and Distributed Applications 152
Integrating Wireless Networks 154
Developing a Strategy 156

Chapter 7 – Le Quiz 161

Appendix A: Answer Keys 165

Appendix B: Publications, Conferences & Additional Reading 173

Index 183

Preface

This book and the live training program that preceded its creation were designed primarily for network managers and others who need to understand network technology so they can apply it to business problems. The straightforward technical tutorial breaks occasionally to allow you to complete checklists or projects and apply the new information to your own network.

I focus on constructing a strong conceptual framework for each subject and use the standards models as an anchor for understanding how all the complex material fits together. To bring a unifying perspective to the subject, I focus on defining terms and concepts in what I consider the "correct" way. For that reason, you may find some words defined somewhat differently here than you are used to. ALL the companies and network managers listed in case studies and horror stories are real; their names and identifying details have been changed to avoid embarrassment and letter bombs.

This book assumes you have completed *Mastering Internetworking* or a similar introduction to basic internetworking technology and terminology. I do not redefine or re-explain what you already know (or should know). You will also notice that I rarely mention vendor names. While products change on a daily basis, this book takes a more generic approach to the subject matter. When you have completed this book, understand the options available and have matched them with your own specific needs, the vendors you need to talk to are available at conferences and in magazine and trade press ads.

Chapter 1 reviews the OSI and IEEE Model layers and their relationship to advanced internetworking topics. This chapter also reviews some popular architectures, including TCP/IP, SNA, XNS, DECnet and Novell. In Chapter 2, we examine bridging standards in more detail: building a spanning tree, developing a source route, calculating how a network reconfigures itself when an transparent bridge port fails, how SRT and SR-TB bridges operate and how bridge performance varies. As an example of Data Link internetworking, we look at different scenarios for connecting SNA/SDLC networks to TCP/IP networks.

Chapter 3 moves up to the routing layer where we look at the new link state protocols (OSPF and IS/IS), networks using multiple routing protocols, subnetting in various network types and wide-area routing. We also look at IP and ISO addressing. Chapter 4 begins with a discussion of NOSs, their purpose in the network and their relationship to other high-level software. We then look at how NOSs can function as part of your internetworking strategy and the nightmares that incompatible systems can create if you don't plan proactively. We also look at client/server computing architectures and their impact on internetworking as well as middleware options.

Chapter 5 moves out beyond the local network to metropolitan and wide-area internetworking: SONET, SMDS, DQDB, frame relay, ATM, B-ISDN. Naturally, space is limited and entire books exist on each of these technologies. The goal here is to provide you with the tools you need to make the best business decisions.

Chapter 6 represents the most exciting, most exasperating and ultimately most business-critical kind of network: the development and management of integrated multi-protocol internetworks. Practically no one really has one of these. The heroics required of network managers I work with who are trying to manage these new beasts commands my utmost admiration. This chapter begins with a discussion of network planning, which includes backbone management. This chapter touches on a wide range of backbone types including collapsed backbones within a router and linking LANs in an intelligent hub. We conclude with a discussion of wireless networks. Chapter 7 is a comprehensive final exam.

When you have completed this book, you can feel confident that you have a thorough grounding in the technology and business issues involved in internetworking. When you have completed the learning phase of using this book, apply the decision-tools to your business.

V. C. Marney-Petix

Acknowledgments

There are a plethora of persons you **cannot** blame for errors I've made in this book, especially Ellen Brigham, Rich Seifert and Thomas Martin. Also unindictable are David Harris, Elyssa Edwards, Charles Brown, Elise Berhinig, Bob Martinez, Rita Lewis, John Lenko, Jennifer Hart, Julie Weiss and Ray Heckman. The most heart-felt thanks of all are owed to my seminar students, even more so than usual in this advanced course. All your enthusiasm and love for the subject has made this course better every time I teach it.

My copy editor deserves a Purple Heart (or maybe a Victoria Cross). During *Mastering Internetworking*, I was (according to her) overly enamored of dashes. Having taken her strictures on the subject to heart, I have (according to her) in this book transferred my dashing compulsion to a parenthetical compulsion. (I don't know what she's talking about. Do you?)

Dedication

In memory of my father
Anthony Joseph Petix
and my friend
Gatha Hesseldon

Gatha was one of the founding members of the "Bay Area Checkbook", a major consumer publication. She fought leukemia with faith, determination, healthy eating, visualization and positive spirits—all the wonderful things I loved her for even before her illness put them to the ultimate test. She lives as fully now as she ever did, in the hearts of all those she touched. My father left me many vivid, sad, disappointing and funny memories, as well as an occasional moment of personal courage and glory. One such moment occurred as he was supplementing my driver ed class by letting me drive his car. A typical New York driver did an obnoxiously typical New York driver thing and I was determined to do it right back, with bells on. "You figure that's what the world needs—one **more** jerk?" he asked me. I've spent the rest of my life trying (with varying success) not to be "one more jerk."

0
Internetworking Review

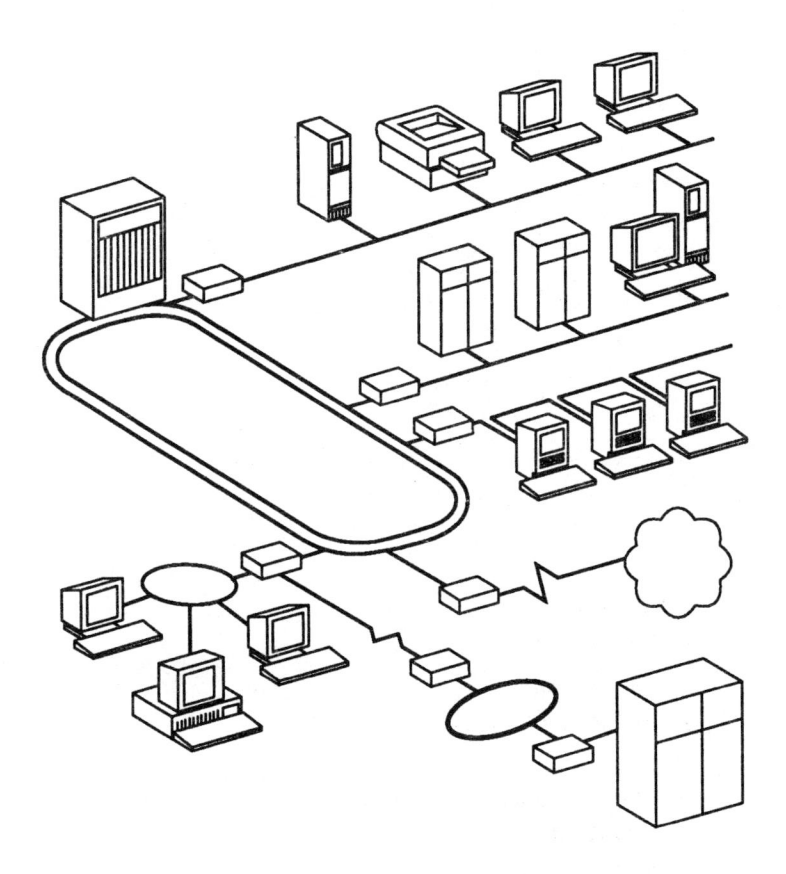

Goals of this Chapter

When you complete this chapter, you will know:
- [ ] How much you know about basic internetworking from your own study or
- [ ] How much you remember from your completion of *Mastering Internetworking*

1. A bridge is a layer _____ device.
   (a) 7
   (b) 2
   (c) 3

2. Routing is protocol-_____.
   (a) specific
   (b) tolerant
   (c) insensitive
   (d) interoperable

3. Routers read the _____ address (header) in a Novell network.
   (a) e-mail
   (b) NetWare
   (c) IPX
   (d) Ethernet

4. The most effective way to reduce overall network operations costs is to minimize _____ costs.
   (a) printer paper
   (b) internet device
   (c) management
   (d) vacation time to net management staff

5. Which network element is smartest?
   (a) smart bridges
   (b) multi-protocol routers
   (c) integrated bridge/routers
   (d) LAN administrators

6. Bridges that receive more frames than they can process will ____.
   (a) use flow control
   (b) drop frames
   (c) fail
   (d) turn red and vaporize

7. How do network managers discover that a bridge is overloaded?
   _____

8. A security-conscious customer should buy:
   (a) smart bridges or routers with filters
   (b) a sophisticated network management system
   (c) routers, for segmentation
   (d) they're all good ideas, it depends

9. If you add Macintoshes to your internet and the internet uses smart bridges on some segments and only IP routers on others, will your Mac users have full access to all other users in the internet?
   (a) No. They cannot communicate with NetWare users.
   (b) Yes, because bridged frames go everywhere.
   (c) No. Routers will block them from some segments.
   (d) No. They cannot communicate with IBM PCs using smart bridges. They need routers.

10. A corporation that plans to use the network as a strategic tool and therefore plans to put mission-critical applications and services on the internet, need high:
    (a) reliability, using routers
    (b) bandwidth, using bridges
    (c) numbers of mainframes and super-minis
    (d) bandwidth, using gateways

11. The best way for network managers to manage the new bandwidth hog devices is to:
    (a) put them all on a single segment, not anywhere else
    (b) distribute them equally on all segments, to even the load
    (c) forbid them to log on except evenings, weekends and holidays
    (d) track traffic patterns; buy equipment and set policies accordingly; protect the core business applications

12. In a network composed of integrated bridge/routers (IP), a Macintosh user exists in a logical:
    (a) routed internet
    (b) bridged LAN
    (c) routed LAN
    (d) Mac/LAN

13. T-1 is:
    (a) a speed
    (b) a new technology
    (c) available only from public networks, like AT&T and Tymnet
    (d) an analog medium

14. A company with on-demand high-bandwidth applications would benefit most from:
    (a) fractional T-1 service
    (b) ISDN's Basic Rate Access (2B+D)
    (c) unsubrated T-1 service
    (d) learning bridges

15. T-1 is 1.544 Mbps:
    (a) all around the world in CCITT countries
    (b) in North America only
    (c) in Japan, Korea and the US only
    (d) in North America and Europe

16. Why is SNMP becoming the network management software of choice for internet devices specifically?

   (a) SNMP is the OSI standard

   (b) Low memory requirements in the managed devices compared to CMIP

   (c) Much more sophisticated than CMIP

   (d) CMIP doesn't work with internet devices, only end user encompassing devices

17. An octet is

   (a) Eight oboes playing Mozart

   (b) Eight violins playing anything

   (c) Just another name for byte

   (d) Eight bits

Internetworking Puzzle

- ☐ Numbers are written out in words.
- ☐ Punctuation (dashes, for example) is ignored.
- ☐ If you think you have one answer figured out but it seems to preclude one or more other answers (pqw can't be an OSI Layer, can it?), think about the questions again. Sometimes you will see another way of approaching the question.
- ☐ Most importantly, go through the puzzle in its entirety once and fill in all the "easy" answers before you try the harder questions.

Enjoy!

Internetworking – The Puzzle

Down
1. Needs an "e"
2. Power source for bridges
3. Soothes a network manager's frazzled nerves with a "meow"
4. ST bridges do _____ bridging.
5. Bridge with a college education
6. Multi-Bus to DISOSS: an _____ gateway
7. Bridges and routers are (abbrev.) devices
8. Fractional, subrated and unsubrated are all options
12. 802 subcommittee number: network management
15. Internal Router (abbrev.)
17. Where engineers gather
20. Network manager's usual mien
21. Provides aspirin to cure 20 down
22. Bridge's response to a "foreign" address
25. Routers balance this
30. "_____ ahead, spend as much as you want," the CFO said. The Network Manager fainted.

Across
2. Power source for routers
5. Frame that every device reads
9. Network status that makes managers smile
10. Frame-exchange layer
11. ATMs use this LAN application
13. When network managers eat lunch at their desk
14. Data _____ Layer
16. Routers are used as this kind of wall
18. How RIP measures "cost"
19. Routers listen for their _____
23. Nice place to buy 8 Down equipment; HQ in Redwood City, CA
24. LAN vendors in the internet market sell _____ -stop shopping
26. Second troubleshooting question: Is it _____?
27. Device must specify a complete path when using _____ routing
28. IEEE standards put a _____ between committee and sub committee numbers
29. 6 down gateway (abbrev.)
31. Internet managers need a can _____ attitude
32. Internet tree

See *Appendix A* for the solution to the puzzle.

1
Architectures Review

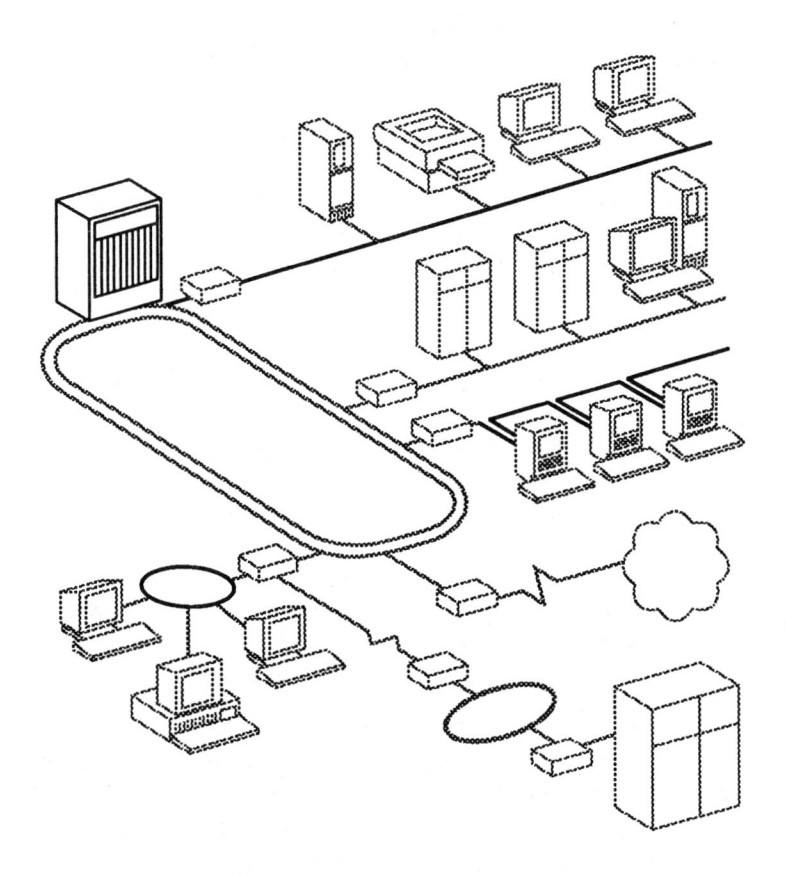

Goals of this Chapter

When you complete this chapter, you will have reviewed:
- ☐ Basic internet device classifications
- ☐ Networking infrastructures, wired and wireless
- ☐ The TCP/IP, SNA, Novell and DECnet architectures

Reviewing The OSI Model

The Open Systems Interconnection (OSI) Model for network architectures includes specifications for seven layers of network functions, from the physical wiring to sophisticated applications support. The OSI Model was originally developed by the International Organization for Standardization (**ISO**) and is now approved by the International Consultative Committee for Telephony and Telegraphy (**CCITT**).

The Physical Layer puts raw bits onto the medium and transports them to their destination. The Data Link Layer organizes bits into frames. The IEEE model divides this into a Logical Link Control (**LLC**) sublayer (**802.2**) and the Media Access Control (MAC) sublayer. The IEEE's 802.1 standard provides for network management and bridging.

You have two standard ways of routing packets between sender and receiver at the Network Layer: virtual circuit service or connection oriented (CONS) and Datagram or connectionless service (CLNS). The Transport Layer provides quality control of the network's data transport function. The Session Layer creates, manages and terminates sessions. When LAN users log onto a server, they are making a Session Layer connection. Presentation Layer services include character code translations (ASCII/EBCDIC, for example) and screen format translations. The Application Layer contains the basic utilities that support the application programs, not the applications themselves.

The illustration shows how the common internet device types fit (functionally) into the OSI Model. Chapters 2 and 3 focus on advanced issues in bridging and routing, respectively. Network operating systems are covered in Chapter 4 while Chapter 5 discusses wide-area options at all the layers. Multi-protocol networking (Chapter 6) poses its challenges at all layers.

Mapping Devices to Layers

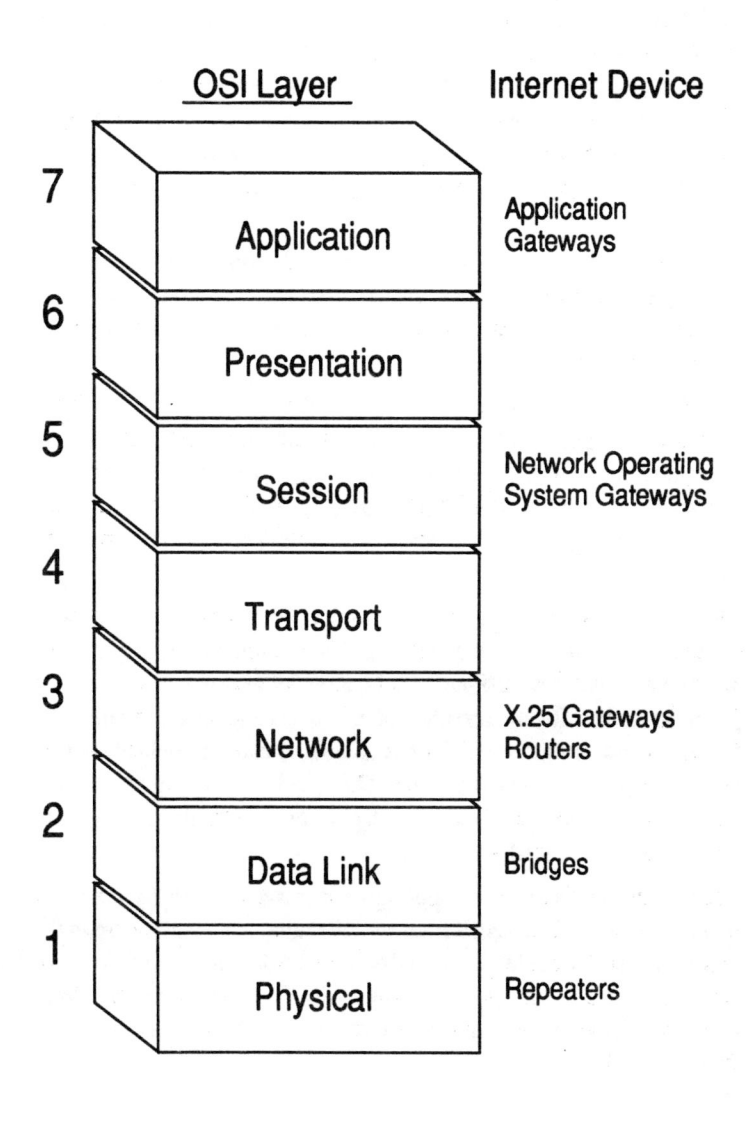

OSI Layer	Internet Device
7 Application	Application Gateways
6 Presentation	
5 Session	Network Operating System Gateways
4 Transport	
3 Network	X.25 Gateways Routers
2 Data Link	Bridges
1 Physical	Repeaters

Network Infrastructures

You can think of networks as composed of a series of infrastructures, beginning with the communication path, either wired or wireless. The most common wiring choices are unshielded twisted pair (UTP) and optical fiber, both glass and plastic. Wireless LANs find their niche in shipping, warehouse and other "nomadic" departments. The topologies employed by the wired LANs generally fall into the star or bus categories and these topologies can be arranged hierarchically, as the illustration shows.

Hubs represent a second layer of infrastructure above the basic wiring. This layer of devices includes hubs, concentrators, fan outs and multiport repeaters. Third generation hubs include integrated bridging, routing and management.

The third layer of infrastructure includes the devices that make internetworking happen, linking separate segments into LANs and LANs into internets. These devices include bridges, routers and gateways. Above this internet infrastructure, we conceptualize the enabling technology for information sharing: servers and their network operating systems.

The highest layer of infrastructure is not as well developed and most solutions come from small companies. These products, as they continue to mature, will revolutionize application delivery to end users. Most products form software kernels that allow transparent information retrieval. These products, referred to as middleware or application kernels, will give networks the "glue" they need to speed up application development and deployment and give end users the ease of use they've been promised for so long.

Prior to the 1990s, most computing took place in relatively homogeneous networks, following a single architecture. Now that we are in the multi-protocol decade, we must be prepared to move information across architecture and protocol boundaries. Let's take some time to review the various architectures involved in this revolution and how they have evolved.

Network Infrastructures

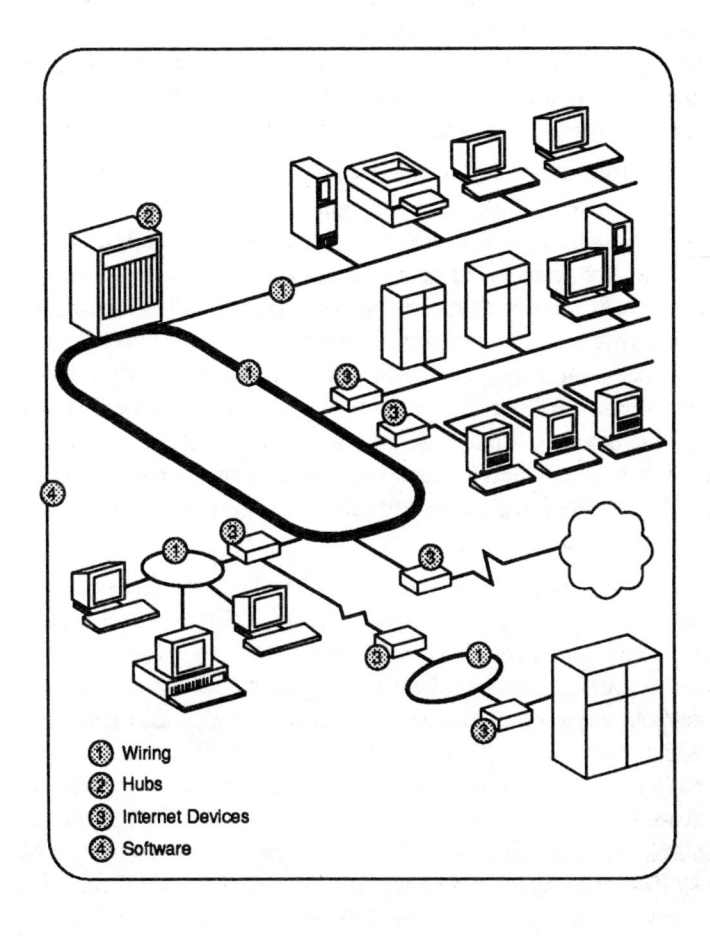

- ① Wiring
- ② Hubs
- ③ Internet Devices
- ④ Software

SNA: New and Old

IBM developed its proprietary Systems Network Architecture (**SNA**) to serve the needs of terminal to mainframe traffic so SNA began its life as a hierarchical network architecture. In the following two decades, SNA has evolved as the computer industry has evolved: from terminals to desktop computers; from hierarchical computing to peer processing; from centralized to distributed topologies and architectures.

In 1988, IBM took a major step toward peer processing with the announcement of the Advanced Program to Program Communication (**APPC**) specification, to eventually replace NetBIOS, and the logical unit (**LU**) **6.2** protocol for peer-peer session services. Peer services means that PCs and workstations can communicate with hosts as peers, without switching to terminal emulation mode. Advanced Peer to Peer Networking (**APPN**) gives End Nodes dynamic directory service, which eliminates the need for labor-intensive static directories in mainframe applications. While IBM has been developing APPN, a coalition of vendors led by Cisco Systems has developed an alternative protocol called **APPI**. We will discuss APPN and APPI in more detail in Chapter 6.

The Systems Applications Architecture (SAA) was the first attempt to create common interfaces across MVS, VM, OS/400 and OS/2 computers, the precursor of what we call middleware today. These common interfaces, called Common User Access (CUA), give users access to data from anywhere in the network using a single "look and feel." IBM's newest venture into middleware begins with Common Transport Semantics (CTS), which allows developers to create applications that are not linked to specific transport protocols. With CTS, you can run SNA emulation across a TCP/IP network to reach a remote SNA host. IBM has a working prototype of CTS called Sockets Over SNA. We will discuss specific aspects of Token Ring and the New SNA in Chapters 2 and 3, middleware in Chapter 4 and SNA interoperability with TCP/IP and other architectures in Chapter 6.

In this book, Token Ring is an IBM product while token ring is a generic term.

New SNA

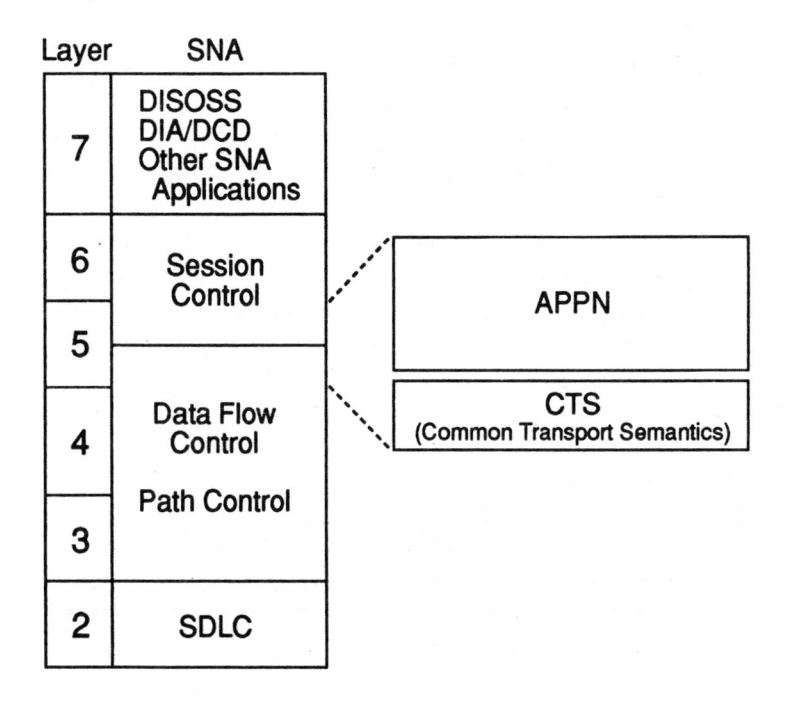

Layer	SNA
7	DISOSS DIA/DCD Other SNA Applications
6	Session Control
5	
4	Data Flow Control
	Path Control
3	
2	SDLC

APPN

CTS (Common Transport Semantics)

XNS, Novell and DECnet

The Xerox Network Systems (**XNS**) architecture begins at the network layer with the Internet Datagram Protocol (IDP) and continues with a transport protocol called the Sequenced Packet Protocol (SPP). XNS protocols influenced the development of other early network architectures as well as OSI.

When Novell began developing its own architecture, it developed a version of IDP called Internet Packet Exchange (**IPX**) and a version of SPP called Sequenced Packet Exchange (**SPX**). Above SPX, Novell developed a network operating system (NOS) called NetWare. We will discuss NetWare in Chapter 4.

Digital Equipment Corporation (DEC) has delivered a wide range of communications products during its years in the computer market, including the Local Area Transport (LAT) protocol. Its major strategic direction and lasting contribution to the evolution of network architectures, however, is DECnet. Digital began **DECnet** as an entirely proprietary solution to the need for VAX–VAX communication, but the architecture has evolved beyond that narrow goal. At layers four through seven in the current DECnet Phase IV, buyers can choose either proprietary DEC protocols or an OSI stack. DEC has begun shipping the latest version of its OSI architecture, formerly known as DECnet Phase V and rechristened **Advantage Networks**. Although many vendors have announced support for OSI products, Digital has come the farthest in actually bringing product to market (doing a brisk business outside the U.S.) and integrating OSI protocols with its proprietary architecture and real corporate business needs. For companies needing an OSI infrastructure, this is probably the most robust solution. Advantage Networks aims to bring SNA, IPX/SPX, AppleTalk, TCP/IP and OSI into a true distributed computing environment.

We will use Advantage Networks as an example of an OSI infrastructure supporting multi-platform networking, as well as how to integrate OSI with proprietary protocols, in Chapter 6.

The Novell and XNS Architectures

Layer	Novell	XNS
7	NetWare	
6		Courier
5		
4	Sequenced Packet Exchange	Sequenced Packet Protocol
3	Internet Packet Exchange	Internet Datagram Protocol

The Internet

In the 1970s, the Department of Defense sponsored the Defense Advanced Research Projects Agency (DARPA) that comprised a collection of subnets run by various agencies, including the Department of Defense, the Department of Energy, the National Science Foundation and NASA. DARPA began working on internetworking technologies and developed a suite of protocols for its ARPAnet, the most important of which are the Internet Protocol (**IP**) and the Transmission Control Protocol (**TCP**). Because the early ARPAnet involved users running primarily UNIX platforms, TCP/IP has always been closely associated with the UNIX operating system. TCP/IP took on a life of its own because it was found to be so usable in such a wide variety of circumstances and a wide variety of applications. It is now one of the most popular commercial protocol stacks in the world.

Today's **Internet** is managed by the Internet Activities Board (**IAB**) which determines general policy. The Internet Engineering Task Force (**IETF**) makes decisions on technical issues. Protocols that are accepted for use on the Internet are proposed and accepted through the dissemination of what are known as Requests For Comment (**RFCs**). The IAB and IETF make final decisions on proposals.

The Internet protocols are shown opposite. IP performs connectionless (datagram) service. TCP provides connection-oriented (virtual circuit) service with User Datagram Protocol (UDP) for connectionless service. The Domain Name Service (DNS) provides the equivalent of directory service (what would be X.500 in OSI). The Telnet protocol gives you remote terminal access. The Internet protocols are evolving rapidly as technology and markets move forward. It is unfortunate that the TCP/IP partisans have spent so much energy battling the OSI protocols rather then spending the same amount of energy working to allow these two stacks to interoperate. In Chapter 6 we will expend some energy discussing interoperating scenarios.

Internet Organization

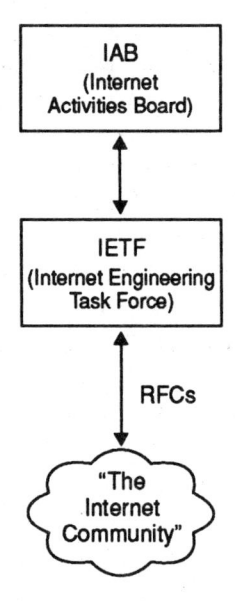

```
        ┌─────────────────┐
        │       IAB       │
        │   (Internet     │
        │ Activities Board)│
        └────────▲────────┘
                 │
                 ▼
        ┌─────────────────┐
        │      IETF       │
        │(Internet Engineering│
        │   Task Force)   │
        └────────▲────────┘
                 │  RFCs
                 ▼
           ╭───────────╮
           │   "The    │
           │  Internet │
           │Community" │
           ╰───────────╯
```

The TCP/IP Protocol Stack

Layer	TCP/IP
7	Telnet, SMTP, SNMP, FTP, DNS
6	
5	
4	TCP / UDP
3	IP

SMTP – Simple Mail Transfer Protocol
SNMP – Simple Network Management Protocol
FTP   – File Transfer Protocol
DNS   – Domain Name Service

Reviewing Internet Devices

Mastering Internetworking introduced you to repeaters, bridges, routers and gateways. **Repeaters** extend the length of the cable plant. **Bridges** process Data Link frames, linking separate LANs into a single LAN. They are blind to upper-layer protocols (except as filtering criteria) and focus primarily on source and destination Data Link addresses. Bridges can drop, forward or flood frames as needed. Bridges are fast, relatively inexpensive and smart ones can perform very complex filtering. Learning bridges dynamically create an address table, adding, changing and aging entries as appropriate.

Routers are protocol specific and can communicate dynamically with end user devices and other routers to build multiple alternate routes and manage traffic loads. We call routers "firewalls" because they prevent local broadcast storms from proliferating. They connect separate networks. Routers are smarter and therefore more manageable and programmable. Filtering and security options are very complex.

A **gateway** re-formats or re-envelopes a packet, performing functions associated with the Network through the Application Layer. (In contrast, a router chooses the best route for a packet but changes only the packet's addressing.) Architecture gateways transform packets from one architectural and protocol stack type to another, almost always at the Network Layer. Application gateways transform a packet's specific application or presentation format to another, usually at the Application Layer.

The devices we studied in *Mastering Internetworking* primarily focused on moving packet-switched data from LAN to LAN. In Chapter 5 of this book, we will expand the discussion to include the movement of voice and video—the extremely time-sensitive **isochronous** traffic. As networks begin needing to move isochronous multimedia traffic, technologies that support isochronous transfer will take a more prominent role in your decision-making.

ARCHITECTURES REVIEW 21

Internetwork Devices

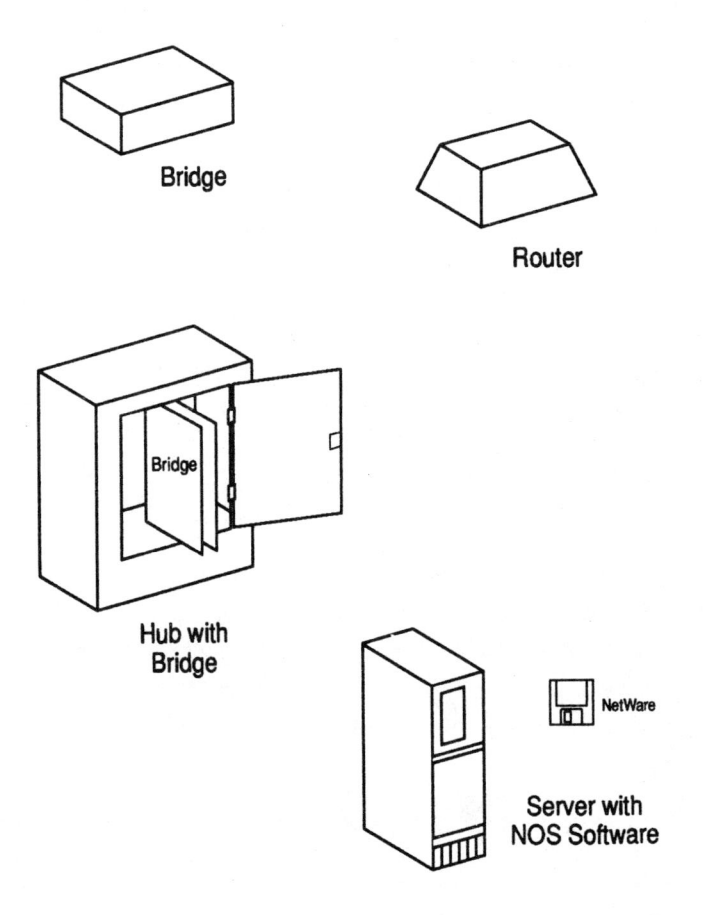

Bridge

Router

Hub with Bridge

NetWare

Server with NOS Software

Key Words

The words and phrases highlighted in **bold** represent key concepts in this chapter. Please take the time now to write down your own definitions of these terms, using the list below and additional paper if needed. Then compare your efforts to the training text. This is an excellent way for you to determine weak points in the breadth and depth of your understanding this chapter.

ISO	repeaters
CCITT	bridges
LLC	routers
802.2	gateway
SNA	isochronous
APPC	
LU 6.2	
APPN	
APPI	
XNS	
IPX	
SPX	
DECnet	
Advantage Networks	
IP	
TCP	
Internet	
IAB	
IETF	
RFCs	

2
Advanced Bridging

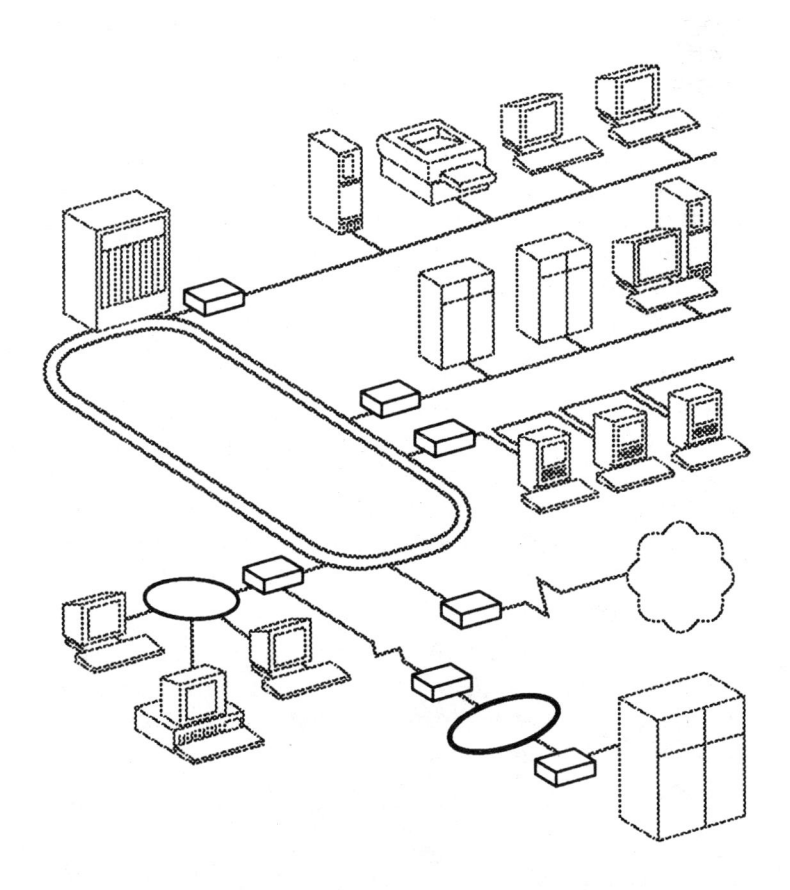

Goals of this Chapter

When you have completed this chapter, you should be able to:
- [ ] List the advantages and disadvantages of spanning tree vs. source route bridging
- [ ] Create spanning trees in bridged networks
- [ ] List the advantages and disadvantages of tunnelling vs. conversion in SNA migration
- [ ] Create a bridging strategy for your network

Kinds of Bridges

Mastering Internetworking introduced you to 4 types of bridges: standalone bridges, bridging software incorporated into a PC or server, integrated bridge/routers and bridging integrated into T-1 multiplexors, LAN hubs and other infrastructure devices. This chapter will take you more deeply into bridging details. We will build a spanning tree, create source routes, show how bridges can help internetwork different architecture types, discuss performance issues and examine tunnelling and conversion in SNA internetworks. In this chapter we will assume that each bridge has 2 or more ports, each of which connects to a different LAN segment. (It's possible to connect more than one bridge port to the same LAN segment.)

As networks become more complex, they are more richly connected. These rich connections are both a blessing and a curse.

Because loops are the scourge of bridges, most of the strategies we'll discuss in this chapter involve preventing loops from occurring. **Transparent** bridges use the spanning tree standard. Source routing transparent **(SRT)** bridges can also handle source routes. Source routing **(SR)** bridges can only source route. The source routing-transparent bridge **(SR-TB)** translates transparent frames into source routed frames. The SR-TB bridge predated the SRT bridge.

The spanning tree calculation allows participating bridges to dynamically discover a single path out of all the available connections that is loop free and still allows all the users to communicate. There must be only one actual path between any two network devices. Bridges calculate the spanning tree essentially by pruning off excess branches (shutting down extra ports). Bridges use configuration messages to communicate with each other and create their spanning tree. (The 802.1 committee calls these **configuration bridge protocol data units.**)

A simplified version of the spanning tree was discussed in *Mastering Internetworking*. Let's move on now to create an actual spanning tree using transparent bridges.

An SRT Bridge

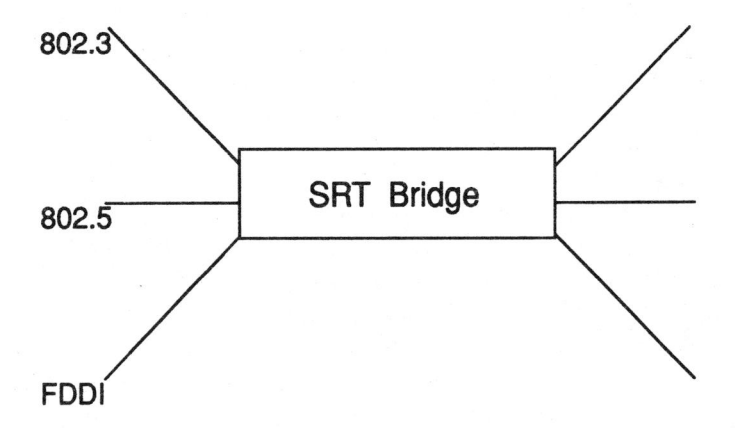

```
802.3 \
       \
        \
         +-----------+
802.5 ---| SRT Bridge|---
         +-----------+
        /
       /
FDDI  /
```

An SRT bridge can handle both transparent and source routed frames.

Configuration Messages

| MAC Header | LLC | Config. Message |

Transparent Bridges

The spanning tree bridges use configuration messages to discover who is the **root bridge** (the one with the lowest ID) and calculate the lowest **cost** path from themselves to the root. If you have more than one bridge connecting two segments and both of them could potentially carry traffic towards the root with the same cost, the one with the lowest ID gets chosen the **designated bridge** for that segment and the others shut down. Each designated bridge has a **root port** that provides the "best path" to the root from that bridge. A configuration message uses the "all bridges" multicast address and a data content of **root ID**, cost and **bridge ID**. Each bridge begins by assuming that it is the root and listens to see if there is another bridge transmitting with a lower cost (better claim to the title). If it believes it is the root, it transmits configuration messages on each port with its ID as the root ID and a cost of 0.

- For each port, the bridge compares its existing outgoing message with the new message it just received. Whichever has the lower root ID is the new root.
- If the root IDs are equal, whichever has the lower cost wins.
- If the new and existing costs are equivalent, then whichever bridge message has a lower bridge ID becomes the new designated bridge. The port identifier is the ultimate tie breaker. (A bridge could receive a message from 2 of its neighbor's ports.) To summarize all this, what a bridge includes in its tree calculation is: the root port plus any other ports that are receiving traffic from another bridge that considers it the designated bridge.

In the illustration, bridge 21 has just been turned on and it is listening to configuration messages on its 3 ports. Bridge 21 hears bridge18 and decides that bridge 16 is the root. (Why?) Then bridge 50 is turned on and 2 minutes later bridge 25 is turned on. Will bridge 21 ever hear a configuration message from bridge 50? From bridge 25? Which bridge becomes the root of this tree?

Who's the Root?

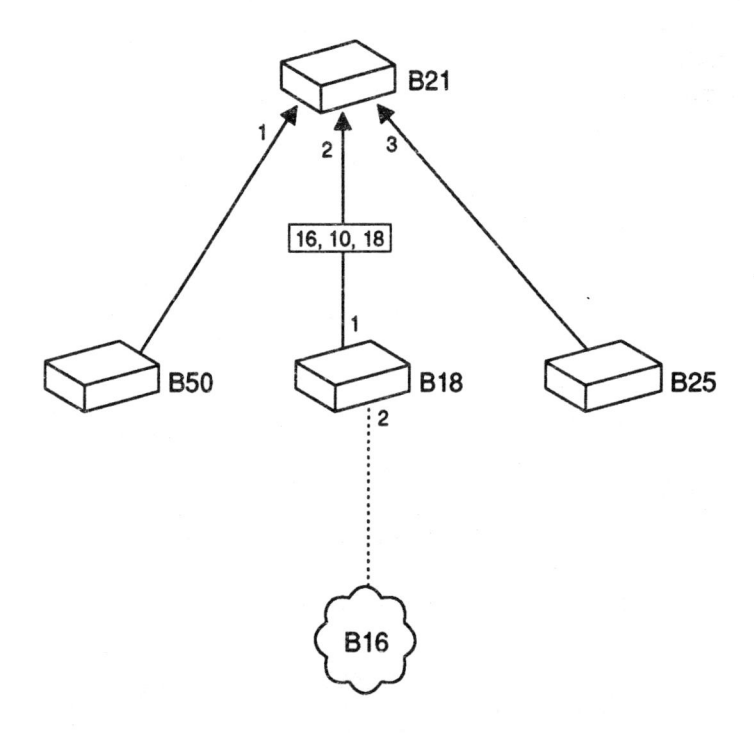

Bridge B21 is receiving a configuration message from bridge 16, via bridge 18. Spanning tree creation is beginning. Bridges 50, 25 and 21 will hear bridge 16's configuration message and decide that it is the root.

Let's Build a Spanning Tree

In the illustration opposite, 11 bridges are collecting configuration messages on each of their ports as they work to build a spanning tree. All Ethernets have a cost of 10, to simplify your calculations. (Different network types generally have different costs.) Each bridge listens to configuration messages to discover who the root is and then propagates the supposed root message onto whichever of its ports is attached to a network that hasn't heard the message. (In other words, the bridge sends the message where it hasn't already gone.) If a better root candidate comes along, the bridge will pass on the new information.

Use a separate sheet of paper to draw the final spanning tree or simply highlight the active path on the illustration opposite.
- What is the root bridge?
- List the configuration message that this root bridge initially sent out.
- Do any bridges have all their ports in blocking mode? If so, name them.
- Which specific ports are in blocking mode among the bridges that are left in the spanning tree?
- If bridge 4 fails, what will the new tree look like?

ADVANCED BRIDGING 29

Let's Build a Spanning Tree

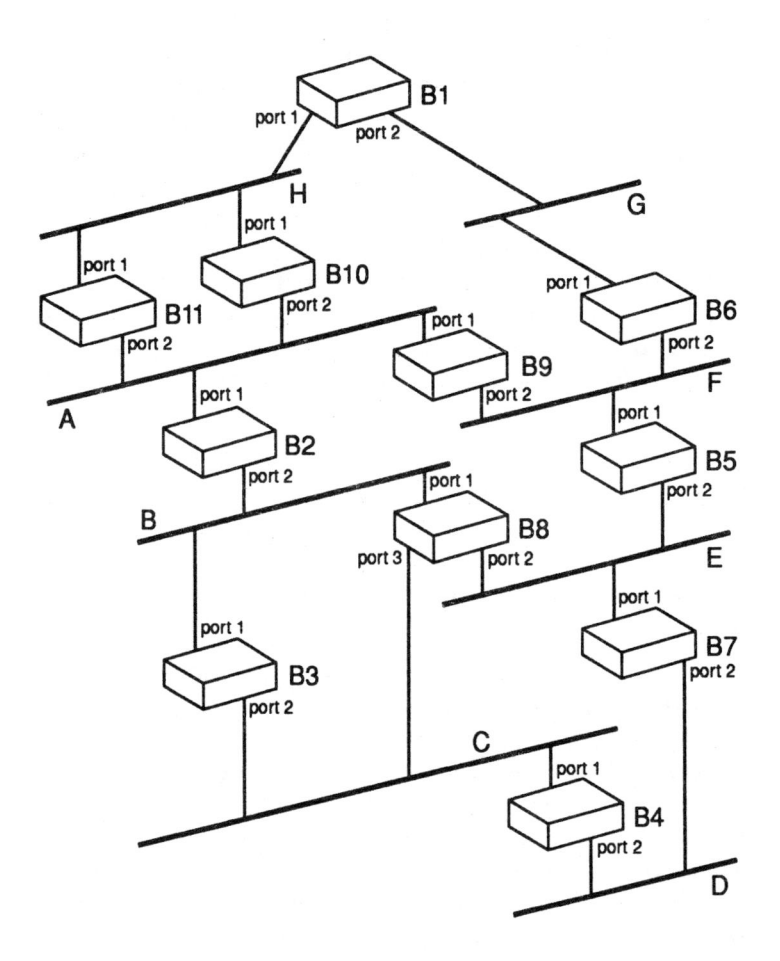

SR, SRT and SR-TB Bridging

In SR bridging, a sender discovers the "best path" to the receiver (a process known as path discovery) and specifies that path in every frame it sends. SR bridges avoid looping by requiring each frame to specify a path; the rest of the network outside of the specified path does not exist. Each 802.5 frame shown here includes a **routing information** (RI) field. The first 3 bits specifies the frame type, either specifically routed, transparent or explorer. All data frames, except multicasts and broadcasts, must be **specifically routed**, so the entire route (up to seven bridges) is listed in the **route field**. The **all paths explorer** frame gets sent out by an end node that is searching for the best path to a specific recipient. A bridge that receives this all paths explorer will add its own address to the list and flood the frame on every port—except the port it came in on or a segment it has already visited, of course.

In an SR network, each bridge must be manually configured with its bridge ID and the IDs of all the LANs it's attached to—a definite hassle. Each corporate network manager creates a unique numbering scheme for bridges and LANs. This leads to loads of fun if two companies try to create an internetwork: there's bound to be duplicate numbers.

So how does an SRT bridge know that the frame is a source routed frame rather than a transparent frame? The multicast bit in the source address is set (=1) in source routed frames to alert the bridge to look for the RI field. The length field tells the bridge how long the RI is (in octets), the direction specifies whether the path should be read left to right or right to left, the frame size field specifies the largest frame that will be able to reach the destination and the route field specifies the path. This field contains up to seven **route designators**, composed of 12 bits of LAN ID and 4 bits of bridge ID. The receiver responds to the first explorer frame it receives. Whichever route involves the shortest round trip delay is usually assumed to be the shortest path and the node will specify this path in the route field of all frames it sends to the receiver.

In general, bridges that will be used only with Token Rings should be pure SR bridges but bridges that might someday need to be part of a multi-protocol internetwork should be SRT.

Four all-paths explorer frames travel from Ilene to Mel

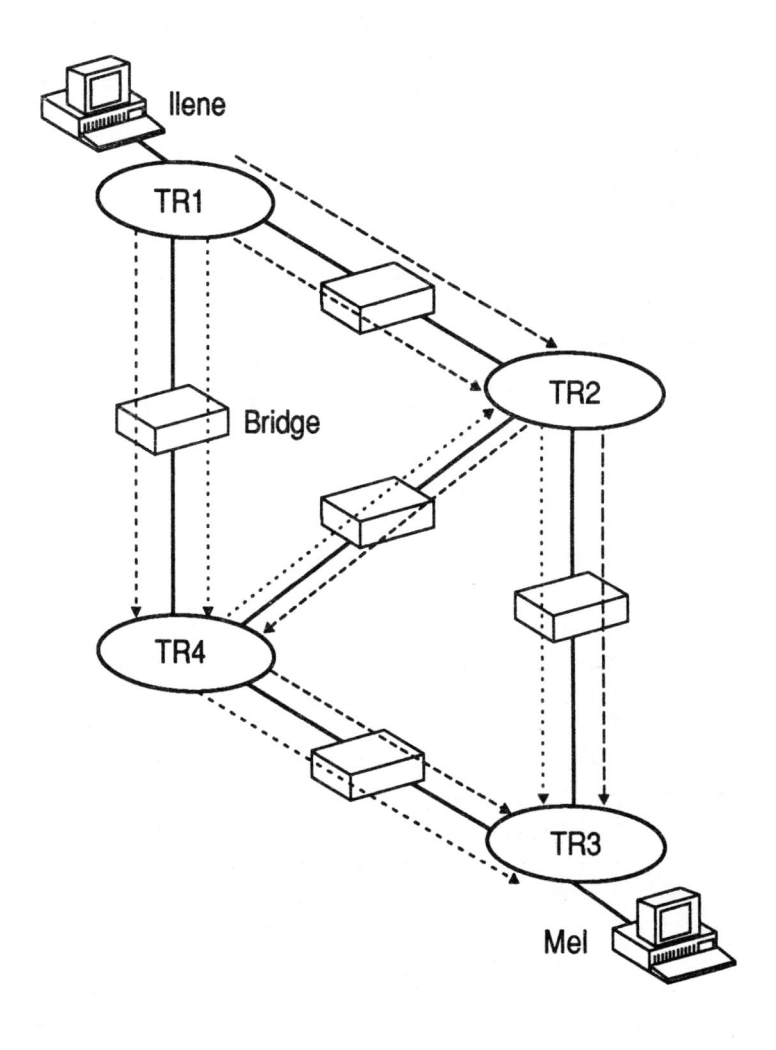

Source Route Bridging Gotchas

#1: Wide-Area Bandwidth

The lower the bandwidth of the connection the more impact explorer frames have on network performance. You can disable your wide-area ports for route discovery or specify a tunnel to a receiving bridge to avoid this problem (if your vendor allows).

#2: Route Aging—Source route bridging isn't dynamic.

Bridges keep caches of routes to specific destinations. How long should a sender keep route information before checking to be sure the route is still valid, much less still best? If you wait too long, changing network traffic patterns can have you using a very congested route in preference to another quicker route. Your connection may fail. If you keep checking at shorter intervals, your explorer frames will create congestion. This is not a parameter that network managers can reconfigure. Whatever aging criteria your vendor chose, you're stuck with, so choose carefully.

#3: SR-TB Bridges

SR-TB bridges can create loops because they are translating information from transparent bridging to source routing. An SR-TB bridge generally will respond to an explorer frame from the SR users on behalf of the end users on the transparent side. The bridge cannot take a transparent frame and forward it on to the receiver on the SR side if it does not have a specific path to the receiver. The bridge will cache the frame and launch an explorer frame to discover a path—if it can. If it is busy with other processing or experiencing congestion, it will drop the frame. SR-TB bridges discover paths to their SR customers by copying paths that come to them from senders and by examining explorer frames. An SR-TB bridge that gets an explorer frame from an SR customer that's looking for a TB recipient, will return an answer to the SR customer, listing itself on the required path and specifying that the TB recipient is on the LAN that the bridge is directly attached to. Note that the TB recipient may actually be three LANs away from the SR-TB bridge.

RI Field with Route Designators

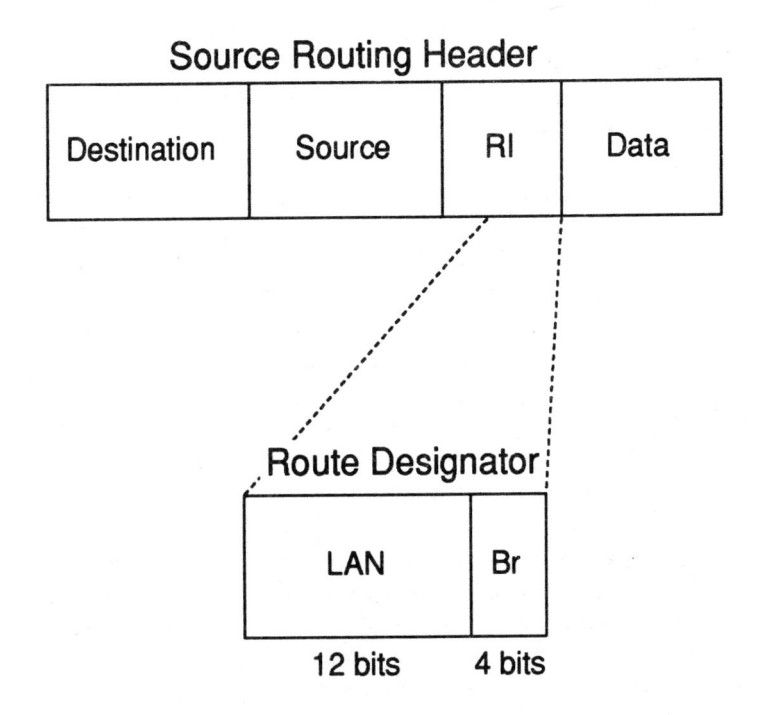

Source Routing Header

| Destination | Source | RI | Data |

Route Designator

| LAN | Br |
| 12 bits | 4 bits |

Bridge Performance Issues

- Congestion is a problem in all networks. What does a transparent bridge do when its neighbors' configuration messages don't arrive? Eventually, if congestion is bad enough and no configuration information arrives and it gets no response to its own message, it changes one or more of its ports from blocking to forwarding. Now you have added looping and total chaos to congestion and user response complaints. (Some analysts, when you ask them for advice on managing a bridged LAN, say "get routers." Now you know why.)
- Don't mix pure SR bridges with pure transparent bridges. The SR bridge ignores frames that don't have an RI field. Transparent bridges ignore frames with RI fields. How do two users communicate if one user produces source routed frames and the other reads only transparent frames? Answer: they don't.
- Use load sharing protocols carefully. The bridges in the illustration lie at the tail end of extensive spanning trees. You might improve response time for the end users attached to the remote LANs if you could shorten this path. What if you connected the remote bridges to each other and allowed them to pass traffic across this link?

The fewer bridges that a frame must traverse, the quicker the trip and the lower the error rate. The terrifying disadvantage of breaking the spanning tree is the possibility of network collapse due to loops. Most such protocols specify that the remote bridges can designate a specific port to send and receive remote traffic destined for a specific other network over a remote link. Only traffic to that specific network will travel out that port and the receiving bridge will not forward traffic anywhere except the target LAN.

In theory anyway. Can you see potential problems with this approach?

ADVANCED BRIDGING

Shortening a Spanning Tree

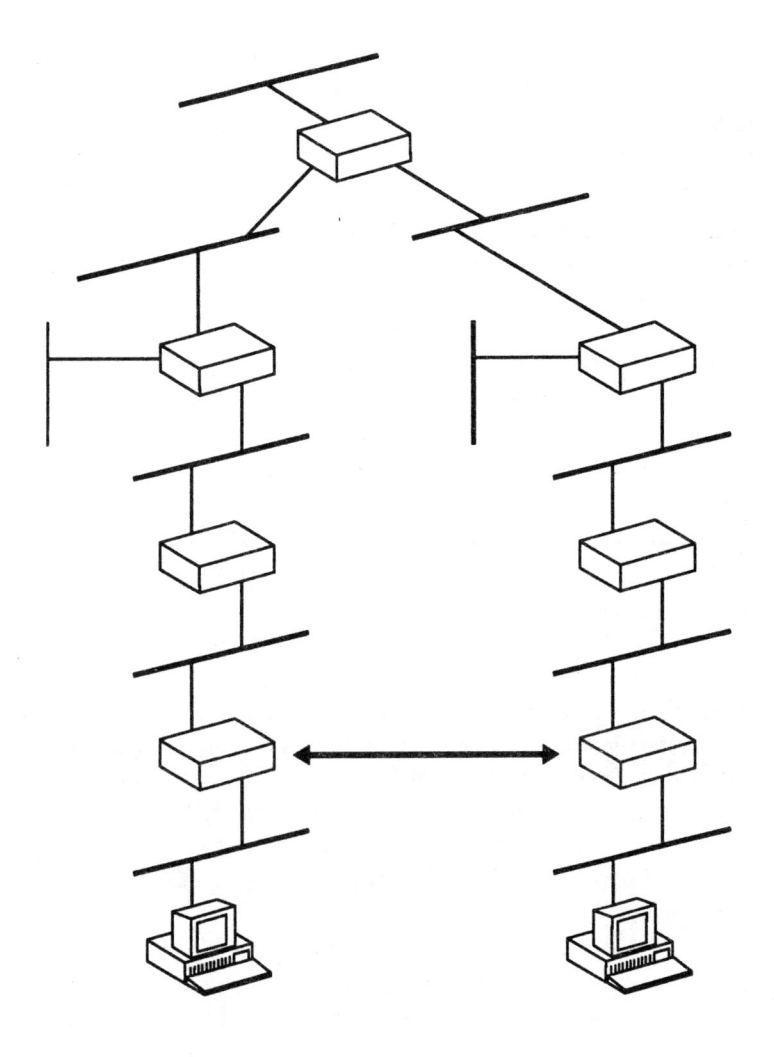

Linking Architectures: Tunnelling/Passthrough

If you want to allow end users in your Ethernet departments to communicate with your token ring users, you will probably buy SRT bridges but this bridge can not by itself ensure that the upper layer protocols are compatible. If a TCP/IP user wants to access information stored on an IBM mainframe, for example, you will need middleware (Chapter 4) or a protocol converter.

To tunnel token ring traffic from one ring to another across an intervening Ethernet/IP network, the internet device puts an additional header on token ring frames to allow them to pass through the IP network. In our example, the sending device puts Ethernet and IP headers on the token ring frames and the receiving device strips the headers again. Tunnelling is also called passthrough. (Some vendors can tunnel with less than the standard 44 byte TCP/IP headers.)

A different problem occurs when an SNA network built on standard Token Rings and 802.2 LLC must internetwork with another SNA network built on IBM's proprietary SDLC. If a Token Ring user needs to create a session to an SDLC host, the ultimate sender and receiver are not using the same protocol, so we cannot tunnel. Conversion is clearly needed here. The converter strips off the Token Ring header and creates a SDLC header or vice versa. SDLC converters have cluster controllers connected to their SDLC side and Token Ring connected to their 802.2 side, as the illustration shows. Vendors refer to **proxy polling** or **poll spoofing** to describe products that will give local SDLC controllers the keep-alives they need to maintain an SNA session. Local polling doesn't waste WAN bandwidth, plus you don't take the chance of timing out and losing the SNA session by actually sending the poll to the mainframe.

For reasons of efficiency and cost savings, many network managers want to merge their routed TCP/IP networks with their existing SNA infrastructure. We will discuss this issue in detail in Chapter 6. SDLC conversion to 802.2 gives you the best choice for long-term planning. Over half a million SDLC controllers constitute a huge installed base of old SNA equipment that no one wants to throw out.

Tunnelling

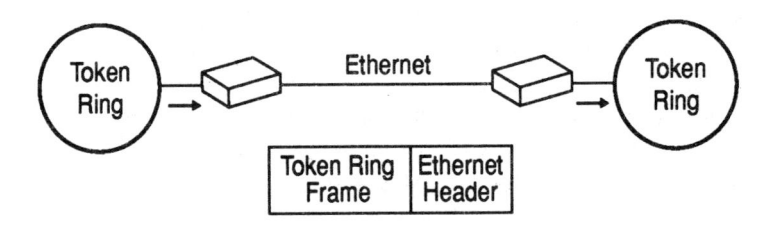

Conversion

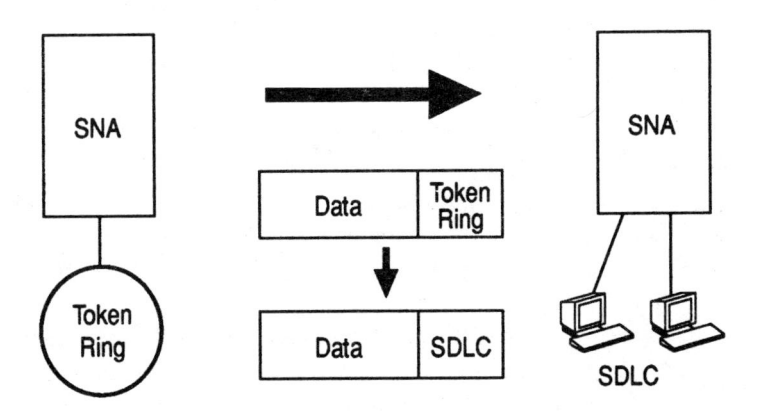

Switching Bridges

The network architecture that we've discussed so far has workgroups connected by bridges or routers, that may connect to larger departmental or divisional groupings and then to a backbone. This hierarchy makes good management sense, especially when implemented with intelligent hubs. The **switching bridge** is basically an attempt to improve user response time (lower the **latency**, in technical terms) in the Ethernet network environment without using traditional bridging technology. The switch isolates each user at the Data Link Layer in contrast to a hub which incorporates only Physical Layer separation (with its integrated repeaters). This means that each user has its own 10 Mbps network. The switch handles packets by switching them from one network to another. An 8 port switch to handle 8 users would take a packet from port 1 and hand it to port 6 while it simultaneously hands a packet from port 3 to port 5. These devices are also known as **Ethernet switches** and switching hubs.

Switching bridges can dramatically improve performance if you have a uniform distributed load—a whole bunch of similar devices putting out equivalent traffic. Switching bridges can improve performance within a workgroup then, where devices are similar and most traffic is peer-to-peer. You can think of this as a return to the advantages of non-shared bandwidth that we had in pre-LAN dedicated lines.

Many network managers find that their servers and mainframes are a performance bottleneck. If LAN bandwidth isn't really the problem, if the problem really is that too any people are trying to make connections to resources through an inadequate number of ports, putting these devices on a switching bridge won't help. What you need in this case is more servers. You can improve access to your global resources—like a server or a mainframe that has company-wide applications or databases—by putting in a good backbone (Chapter 6) or boosting the bandwidth of your infrastructure (Chapter 5).

A Switching Bridge

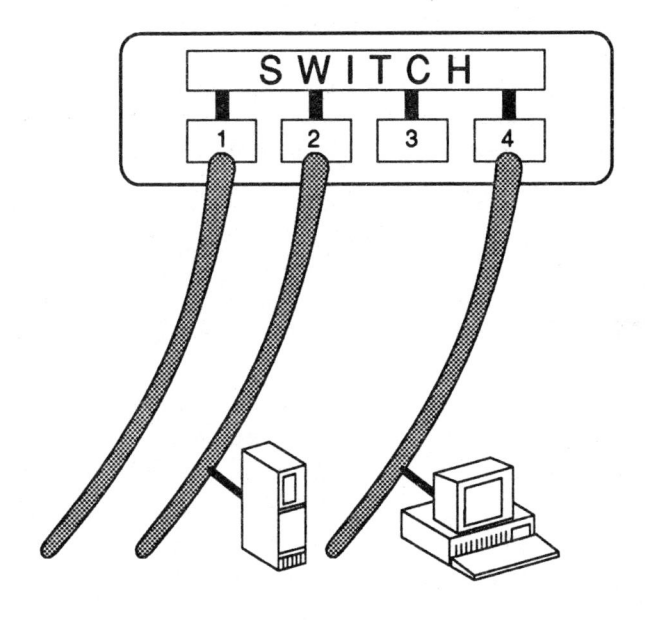

A switching bridge connects 3 Ethernet segments. Each user has their own segment.

Future of Bridging

Standalone bridges, which used to be hot sellers, have been replaced in many large networks by integrated bridge/routers, a trend that includes bridging boards in LAN hubs and WAN switches, particularly T-1 muxes. In addition to the migration of bridging functions to the board level, bridges themselves are becoming more powerful, with more and more sophisticated filtering. As this chapter has discussed, bridging has intrinsic limitations that are fuelling the growth of the routing market.

Many analysts believe that the switching hub is an intermediate step in the evolution towards high-speed collapsed backbones on customer premises and integration with new high-speed public services. In the near term, switching bridges will have an important role to play in networks with traffic intensive applications—but read Chapter 5 before you make any final decisions!

Bridging is not the only Layer 2 function you can indulge in. The migration of SNA networks from SDLC to Token Ring LLC means a burgeoning market in conversion products. Passthrough for SNA to TCP/IP connections, while probably not the most effective long-term solution, continues to spark considerable market interest as well.

In summary, networks of less than 100 nodes and without wiring hubs, have no need to consider anything other than a standalone bridge. If your network is connected or will someday be connected to a larger network, a network using different protocols or extensive wide-area connections, a wiring hub with integrated bridging will cost you less long-term and make your network easier to integrate with other networks. Very large networks with more than 5000 users really should be using bridging and routing that is integrated into a managed hub (SNMP) or else high-performance bridge/routers with a hierarchical series of backbones to keep reliability as high as possible. It's that middle tier—the networking "grey zone" of 100–5,000 workstations—that drives its network managers crazy and keeps consultants in business.

Bridges
Integrated in Hubs and Concentrators

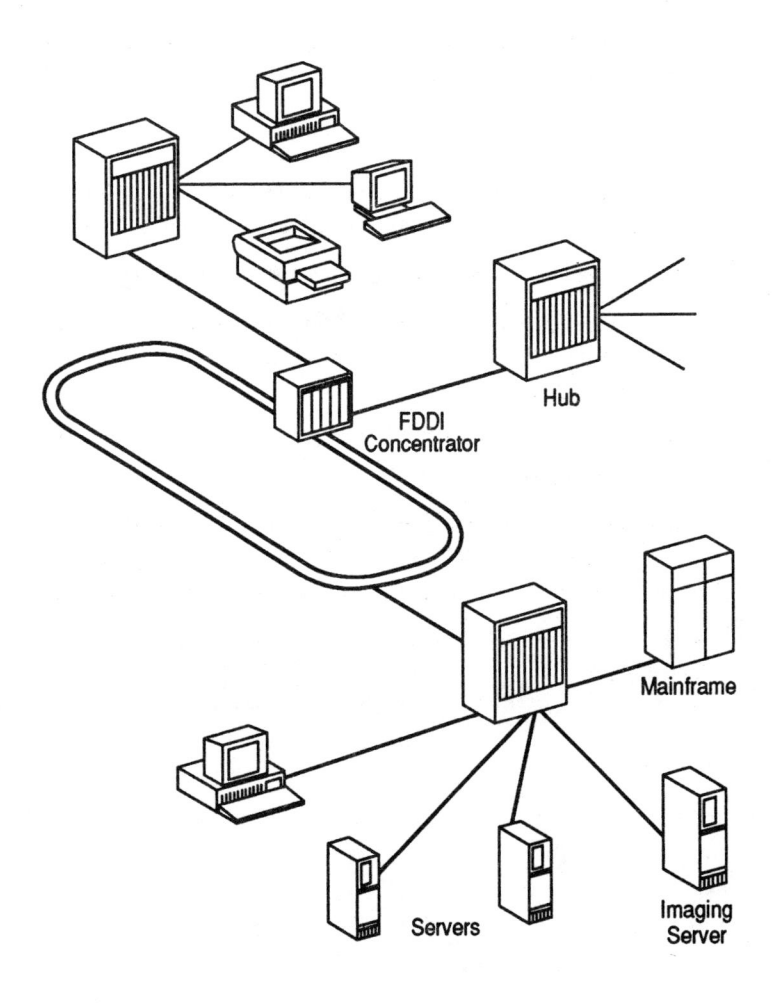

Summary

- Transparent bridges use the spanning tree to prevent loops while source routing bridges must be given a specific path for each frame.
- Transparent bridges choose a root bridge and then calculate a spanning tree from that root, pruning excess branches from the tree by shutting down ports that do not yield the lowest cost to the root.
- SRT bridges handle both transparent and source routed frames.
- Source route bridges discover paths between sender and receiver using all-routes discovery frames. These frames waste significant bandwidth in large networks.
- Switching bridges can improve performance in Ethernet workgroups with uniform distributed load.
- SNA networks can communicate with TCP/IP networks using either tunnelling or conversion. SNA timeouts can be prevented using "poll spoofing" and similar techniques.
- SDLC to LLC conversion offers the best long-term SNA migration strategy.

Review – Chapter 2

1. A source routed frame has a field that a transparently bridged frame doesn't need. What is its name? What does it do?
2. How does an SRT bridge know whether a frame is source routed or transparent?
3. The process by which a token ring node discovers the best path to another node is called _____ _____ _____?
4. Name two challenges associated with source route bridging.
5. Name two challenges associated with SRT.
6. The device that translates traditional SNA to Token Ring is converting SDLC frames to _____ frames.
7. If your global servers are choking on traffic, a switching bridge will (not) improve performance.
8. List two good reasons for trading in your bridges for routers. List two good reasons for upgrading your bridges to integrated bridge/routers. List two good reasons for leaving your network as it is.
9. You have a Layer 2 device that can do SRB and SRT bridging, SDLC passthrough, and IP routing. Will this device connect an SNA network to an IP/Token Ring network?
10. A product that will give local SDLC controllers the keep-alive frames they need to maintain a session are engaging in _____.
11. Switching bridges are most useful for _____ distributed traffic load, such as within a (workgroup/enterprise).
12. _____ bridges are being replaced by SRT bridges because they can cause unintended loops.
13. Spanning tree calculations begin with a _____ bridge which is chosen because it has the (lowest/highest) bridge ID.
14. A bridge port that another bridge considers a root port must remain in (forwarding/blocking) condition.
15. The source route path limit is _____ bridges.
16. Why does this limit exist? Couldn't it be increased?
17. A network manager should block source route broadcasts on (local/WAN) ports.

Key Words

The words and phrases highlighted in **bold** represent key concepts in this chapter. Please take the time now to write down your definitions of these terms, using the list below and additional paper if needed. Then compare your efforts to the training text. This is an excellent way for you to determine weak points in the breadth and depth of your understanding of this chapter.

transparent
SRT
SR
SR-TB
configuration bridge protocol data units
root bridge
cost
designated bridge
root port
root ID
bridge ID
routing information
specifically routed
route field
all paths explorer
route designator
route aging
proxy polling
poll spoofing
switching bridge
latency
Ethernet switches

3
Advanced Routing

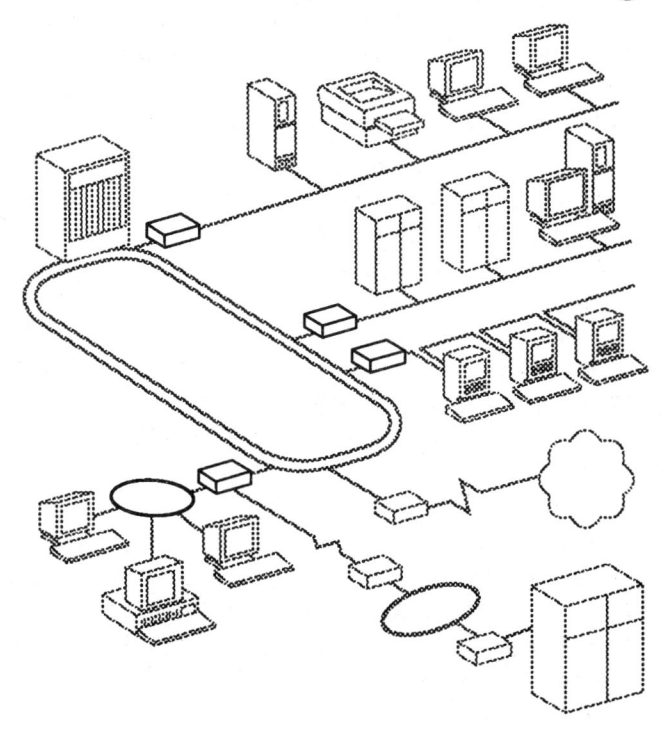

Goals of this Chapter

When you have completed this chapter, you should be able to:
- [ ] List the advantages of link state routing over distance vector routing
- [ ] Name the two most popular link state protocols
- [ ] List two forms of multi-protocol routing and the business benefits of each
- [ ] Create a network design using subnetting

Modern Routing Technology

Through the 1980s, network managers evaluated routers on throughput, measured in packets per second per processor. Router performance measures have improved dramatically in the past 5 years. Many routers use RISC processors and are capable of processing as many packets as their attached networks can present (at "wire speed"). In the 1990s, the battleground has become the numbers and interoperability of the protocols (IP, IPX, etc.) each router can handle.

In addition to network protocols, routing protocols constitute a hot competitive issue. RIP, with its maximum hop count of 16 and **slow convergence**, has needed a replacement for some time. (Routers converge on a new topology following a failure.) The competition in the IP and ISO worlds now runs hot and heavy between the two likeliest successors: **OSPF** for IP and **IS/IS** for OSI. Both these new routing protocols claim to create topology maps with smaller routing databases, less bandwidth dedicated to router synchronization, fewer errors and faster convergence. In addition, a lively debate is raging over how to use multiple protocols in the same network. We will examine all of these issues in this chapter.

Over 50 vendors sell integrated bridge/routers. The market for routing on cards integrated into hubs has grown 90% a year through the first two years of this decade. Some network managers are using the router backplane as a backbone, linking local networks together without sending traffic to a core backbone. (We will discuss these collapsed backbones in Chapter 6). Router backplanes routinely carry between 300 Mbps and 1 Gbps.

This chapter will introduce you to the new routing protocols, how they work and how to use them, subnetwork management, wide-area performance, SNA routing and some advice on how to avoid a starring role in the next networking horror story.

ADVANCED ROUTING

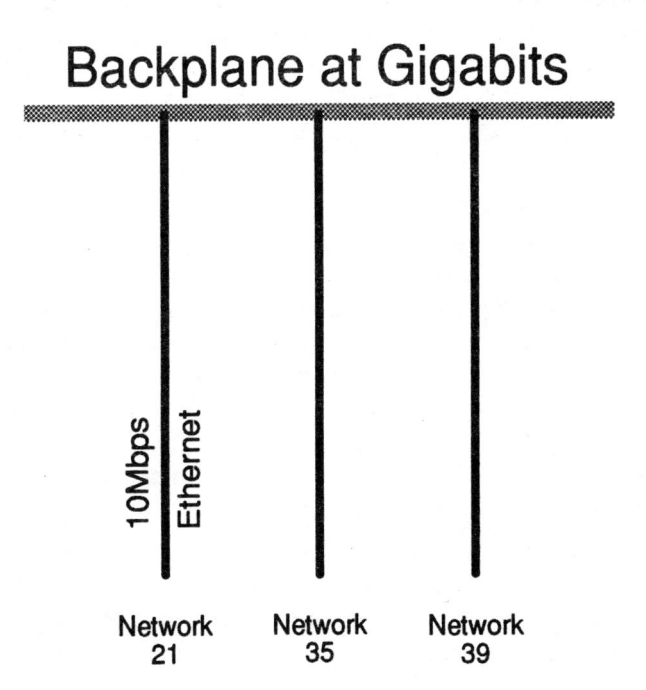

Backplane at Gigabits

10Mbps Ethernet

Network 21   Network 35   Network 39

Problems With Distance Vectors

We discussed **distance vector** routing and the RIP protocol in *Mastering Internetworking*. Tables of routing information specify a reachable network, the address of the router that is advertising the network as reachable and the cost (distance) in hops. Routers listen for routing table information and pass along everything they hear to their neighbor routers. Protocols like RIP and Cisco's IGRP use holddown and split horizon to speed up convergence and/or avoid **counting to infinity**. We say that distance vectors count to infinity when computing a topology. Let's see how this works.

If router B fails, router A will throw out the distance vectors to networks 29 and 33 that it received from B but it will not necessarily conclude that these networks are **unreachable** from routers C and D. In the illustration, B is the only physical connection to network 33. Router A will continue trying to send traffic to networks 29 and 33 through routers C or D until the hop count expires and router A concludes that routers C and D also cannot pass traffic to 29 and 33. The count to infinity issue refers to hop count; infinity is 16 in RIP. Routers A and D or A and C count to infinity until the hop count expires.

Router A doesn't really understand the topology well enough to conclude that network 29 is unreachable through *any* router as soon as router B fails. The same problem occurs if network 29 fails. Again, router A will not understand that network 29 is truly unreachable.

The **holddown** timer sets a period of time after receiving bad news about a link; during this time, the router will not accept good news from the same sender. This reduces the risk of wild oscillations if routing updates arrive out of order—a common occurrence when congestion gets severe. In **split horizon**, routers don't propagate reachability information back to the router that it originally came from. This prevents information loops in which correct information is overwritten by a garbled version of the same information.

Counting to Infinity After Failure

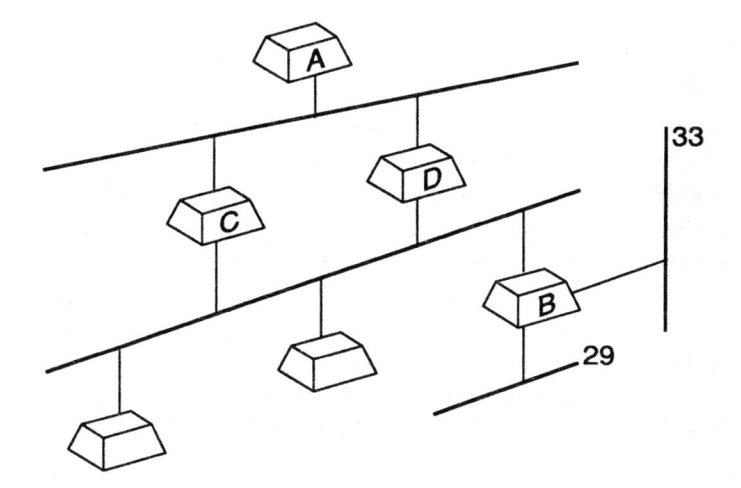

Link State Routing

Instead of trying to fix distance vector protocols, with their intrinsic flaws, we ultimately need to migrate to link state routing. **Link state** protocols converge on a complete network topology map more quickly than distance vector protocols, so these routers can reroute faster around failures and congestion. These protocols also waste less bandwidth on inter-router traffic. We discussed IS/IS and OSPF in *Mastering Internetworking*. Now let's look at OSPF in detail.

OSPF is divided into three parts: **link state flooding**, Shortest Path First (SPF) calculation and **neighbor discovery**. OSPF begins with each individual router flooding other routers with information (**advertisements**) about its *own* connections to the LANs it is directly connected to—information that it can guarantee is accurate. We call these link states (literally, the state of the router-network link). As routers collect these link states from other routers, they create a logical **topology map**. A router uses the SPF calculation to determine the shortest (fastest) path to a distant network. (A path is a collection of router addresses, defining the route that the packet will take.)

Routers use the **HELLO** protocol to communicate with their neighbors. A router's **neighbors** are directly attached to the same networks that it is.

Routers using link state protocols are organized into collections of attached networks variously called **areas, domains** or **autonomous systems** (AS). In OSI terms, a domain can include multiple areas. Routers *within* an area elect one of themselves to be the **designated router**, with whom they all synchronize their maps. The path from each router to its local designated router is called an **adjacency**. We say that link state synchronization and updating occurs only along adjacencies.

Neighbor discovery and LSPs

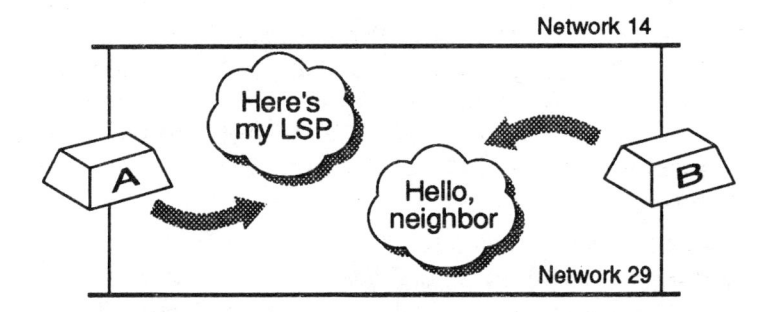

Synchronization

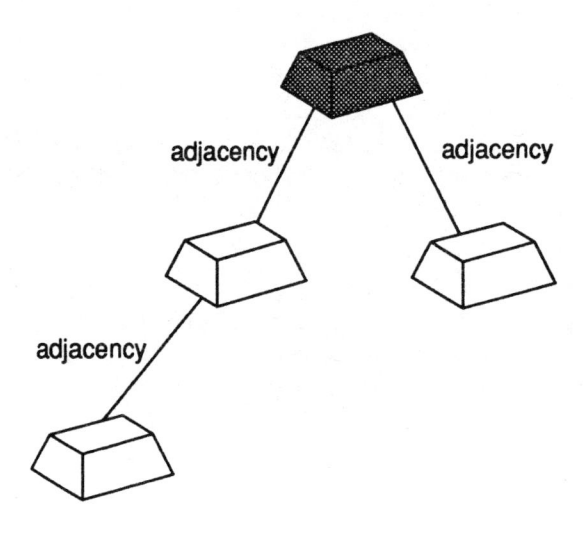

Link State Routing In Detail

Neighbor greeting is how routers discover each other. The OSI IS/IS greeting is called a HELLO. Routers generate link state packets (**LSPs**) or link state advertisements (**LSAs**), depending on which link state protocol they are using. Routers generate LSPs when they have new link information to share, at predetermined intervals (like a keepalive) and whenever they receive a new neighbor HELLO that they have to pass on. New link information includes a link failure, restoration or change in cost (upgrading a 9.6 Kbps line to T-1, for example).

How does a router know if an LSP that has just arrived is really new information or simply took a long route to its destination? LSPs, like other packets, can arrive out of order. A global **time stamp** adds complexity, hardware and therefore cost. When a router fails, its first task on restart would be to request the time, before generating any LSPs. Most link state protocols use **sequence numbers** to alert each other to out-of-order LSPs. If the sequence number of an LSP isn't greater than the number attached to your current information, you ignore the LSP —it's old information. This isn't a panacea either. If a core router fails and your network partitions from the rest of the internet, your local networks will continue operating and your local routers will continue incrementing their sequence numbers. If the core router stays down for a significant amount of time, the local routers' sequence numbers may be considerably greater than they should be when you rejoin the internet. Remote routers may reject LSPs if the gap is too large. The newest protocols use a combination of sequence numbers and time, to try to prevent this confusion.

In the illustration, router A is the designated router. As the routers share their LSPs, the true logical map emerges. The best route to H, for example, changes from "through D" to "through E", the best route to C changes from "through A" to "through B" and so on.

Creating A Topology Map

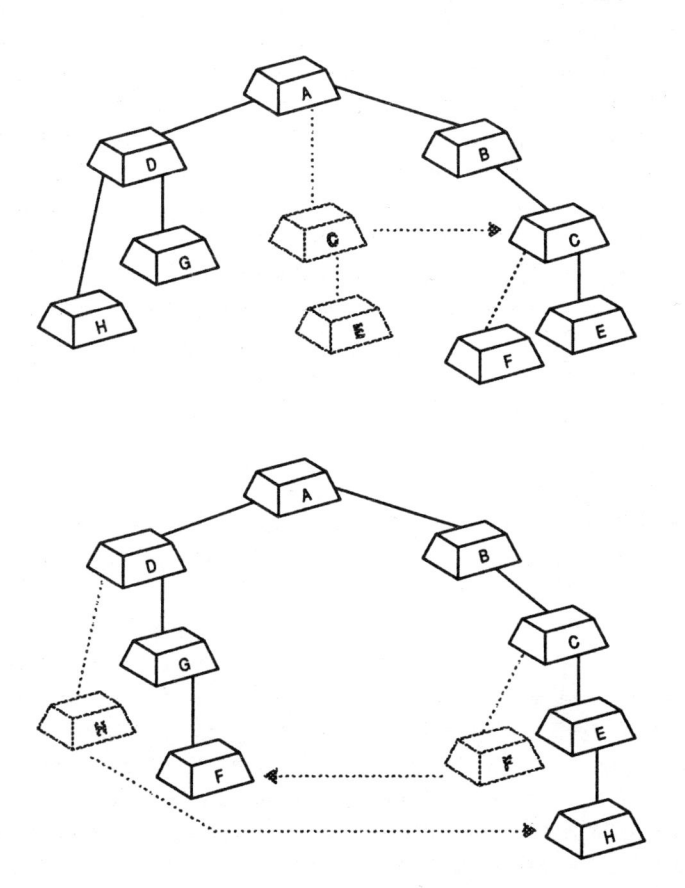

Subnetting

Subnetworking gives your network a hierarchical structure that makes it both flexible and manageable. In the illustration, you can see routers designated **local** (level 1) **routers** within areas 10, 13, 12, 17. These share information about local links and user devices within their area. This saves a lot of unnecessary traffic, since most traffic occurs within the area. **Level 1 routers** pass on area information to level 2 or **border routers**. These **level 2 routers** communicate only with other level 2 routers and their updates concern the links between themselves. What are called areas, domains or autonomous systems (depending on the routing protocol) communicate with each other through level 2 routers. Routing within a domain is **intra-domain routing**. Level 2 routing is called **inter-domain routing** and may use different routing protocols. A level 1 router is also known as an **internal router** while level 2 routers are variously known as **external**, backbone, inter-domain, inter-area and **inter-AS** routers.

You can see how this hierarchical structure helps your network manageability and decreases router traffic. Level 1 routers are responsible for maintaining link state directories for the local networks and pass on routing requests for non-local networks to the level 2 routers. The border routers are not bothered keeping track of local information.

If you have enough traffic to warrant subnetworking into domains, create your domains carefully. The most obvious subdivisions will be on departmental or divisional lines, especially if these groups have their own local LAN administrators. Most traffic is within user communities with a common interest and a department certainly qualifies. You may need to create multiple domains within a department if you have large numbers of users or devices (a very technology-intensive department, for example) or high traffic levels (as with a graphic publishing or CAD/CAM group). Your domains exist to allow you to group networks and apply single routing criteria or commands to them, as well as acting to reduce out-of-domain traffic so consider this as well as you create domains. For instance, you might create a domain composed of one building's networks, even if a department spreads across two buildings in a campus, simply because you want to reduce unnecessary inter-building traffic running on a relatively slow backbone.

Creating Areas

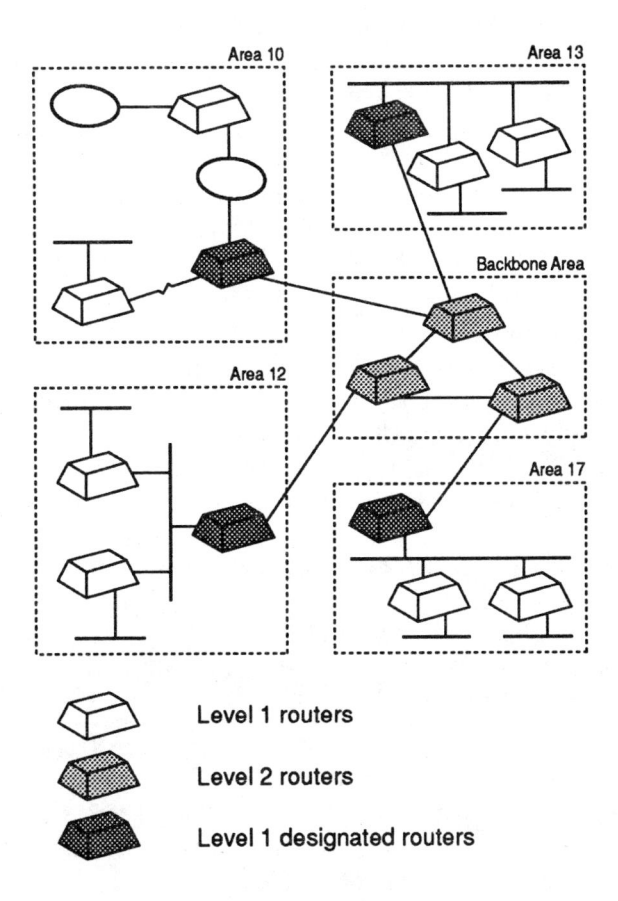

Diagram showing network areas (Area 10, Area 12, Area 13, Area 17, and Backbone Area) connected with Level 1 routers, Level 2 routers, and Level 1 designated routers.

- Level 1 routers
- Level 2 routers
- Level 1 designated routers

This network manager could have used her designated routers as the backbone. She chose level 2 routers to maximize reliability. See Chapter 6 for more on backbone choices.

Inter-Domain Routing

The Exterior Gateway Protocol (**EGP**), a distance vector protocol, allows areas to communicate through a single **core** routing network that connects these areas together. Areas cannot connect to each other except via the core, to which they can have only one connection. A level 2 router using EGP reports to its neighbors on whether a specific destination network is reachable. If you consider that EGP was developed for the Internet core network, this makes perfect sense. These routers report to each other on which local networks at their site are reachable. The Internet core is a collection of routers scattered throughout the world that communicate only with each other concerning the status of the local networks they are responsible for.

The new Border Gateway Protocol (**BGP**) removes the concept of a core by allowing areas to interconnect with each other without going through a central backbone core. It also has the ability to filter more extensively, and to control how the areas may pass data to and through each other. The IETF has approved BGP to ultimately replace EGP in the Internet. Instead of sharing cost information, like EGP does, BGP sends a sequence of AS numbers in the path to the destination network. In other words, BGP lists the route to the destination. This precludes the counting to infinity and slow convergence problems associated with other distance vector protocols. If you remember that the Internet community calls routers gateways, these protocol names make more sense.

The Inter-Domain Routing Protocol (**IDRP**) is another distance vector inter-domain routing protocol derived from BGP and adapted by ISO and the CCITT. It will ultimately support both ISO and IP addresses. An IDRP router is called a Border Intermediate System (**BIS**). A collection of areas is called a **confederation**.

ADVANCED ROUTING

EGP

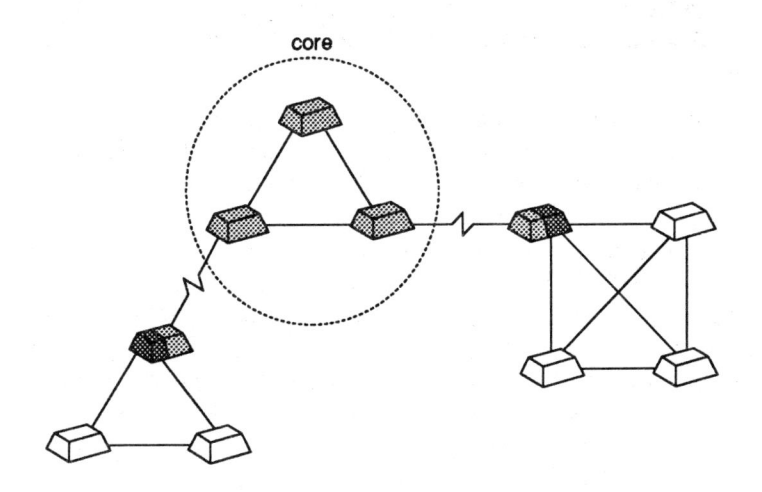

BGP

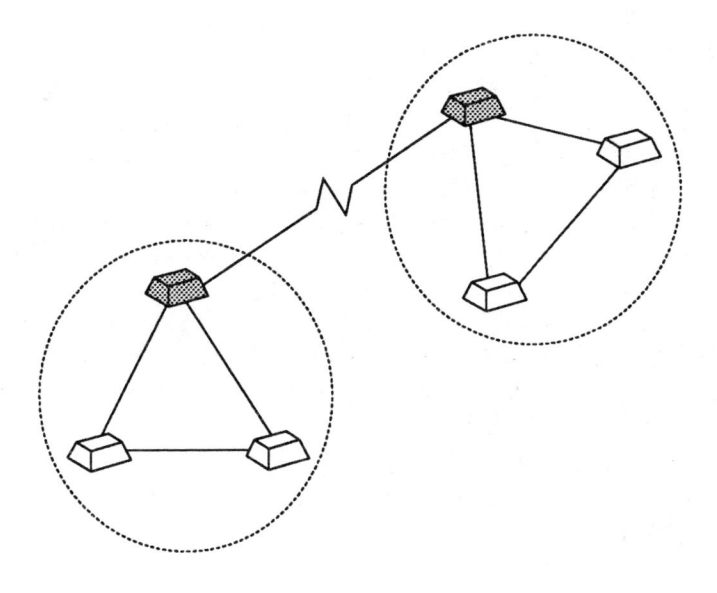

OSI and IP Addressing

In order to understand some aspects of routing, it's helpful to understand Network Layer addressing in both OSI and IP terms. Let's begin with IP.

IP includes **classes of address** starting with class A for large networks like the Internet, class B for campuses and class C for small networks. In the illustration you can see that a class A address allocates fewer bits for the **network ID** (there are very few of these networks) and more bits for the **host ID** while in class C addresses the host ID field is the smallest. (Remember that IP refers to all network devices as hosts.) In a small network you don't need more than eight bits to include everyone's device. The classes can be distinguished by the first three bits in the address. IP has 32 bit addresses, with each of the four octets written in decimal with decimal points between them; this is called dotted decimal notation. If a field includes all zeros, it means "all," as in all devices on a network. In the illustration, you can see area 21 containing local networks 2, 5 and 6. The * in the host field means all hosts in the network.

OSI defines two kinds of Network Layer addresses: a **Network Entity Title** (NET), which a device generally has only one of, and one or more **Network Service Access Points** (NSAP), which are service interfaces to the Transport Layer. In the illustration, you can see the initial domain part (IDP) of the address, which specifies the numbering plan (E.163 for telephony or X.121 for CCITT standard networking) the rest of the address uses. The domain specific part (DSP) is composed of area, the station ID, which is the local address in the area, and the selector. The selector specifies which logical process or entity within the device is using the Network Layer. Most DSPs in the U.S. use GOSIP formatting. The various NSAPs a device has must not differ from its NET except in the selector. Each router in an area keeps track of the hosts in its area by their 6 octet station ID.

Addresses specify a network connection so if you have a connection to more than one network, as a router certainly does, you have one address for each connection.

IP Addressing

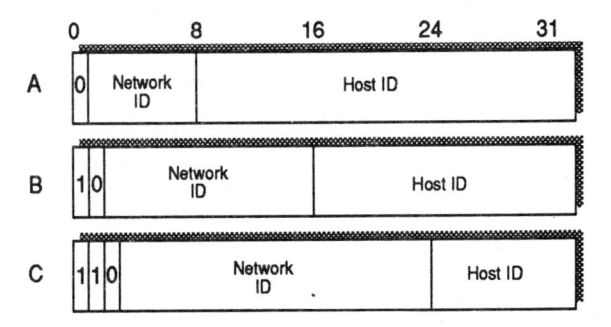

```
      0        8          16          24        31
A   [0| Network ID |            Host ID             ]
B   [1 0| Network ID    |          Host ID          ]
C   [1 1 0|      Network ID          |   Host ID    ]
```

OSI Addressing

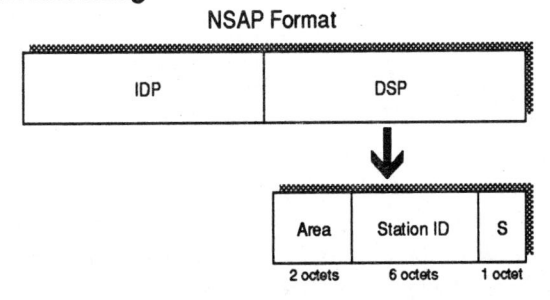

NSAP Format

| IDP | DSP |

Area	Station ID	S
2 octets	6 octets	1 octet

Local Networks 2, 5, and 6 within area 21

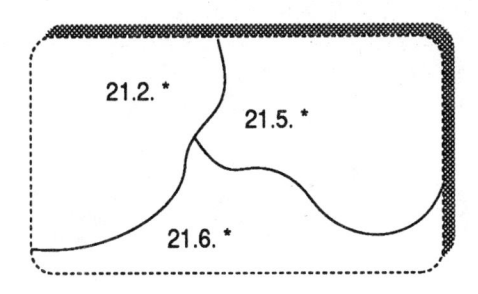

- 21.2.*
- 21.5.*
- 21.6.*

Multiple Routing Protocols

Most network managers do not deliberately set out to drive themselves crazy by setting up networks whose routers run more than one routing protocol. A company may acquire a new subsidiary with an incompatible network, departments that used to be autonomous will be added to the corporate internetwork, a company may want to connect to a supplier's or customer's network and corporate alliances may force two networks to merge. Insisting that your routers run different protocols is a sure recipe for disaster in the short term. On the other hand, it is your duty as a network manager to ensure that your network has the flexibility to deal with corporate changes, so some compromise needs to occur.

Translating from one protocol to another is a process known as **redistribution**. A router that redistributes routing information runs both protocols and usually lives on the border where one protocol's domain touches another's. Each routing protocol measures its cost differently and these costs never translate exactly. For instance, how would you convert hop count (RIP) into round-trip delay (HELLO)? Most redistribution schemes use a standard list of values so each hop equals a few thousand milliseconds of delay, for example.

Life gets really interesting when you try to redistribute distance vector cost into link states. In the case that follows, a network includes both RIP and OSPF domains and a network manager who decides to redistribute between them. In fact, this constitutes our first Horrible Case (I wanted Case Study; the editor wanted Horror Story; we compromised): **redistribution loops**.

Redistribution can create routing table loops if redistribution ends up translating from RIP to OSPF and then back to RIP, for example, because the cost may not be translated back to RIP properly. In the example shown, a router in RIP 1 could learn of connections to a network in RIP 2. Routers 11 and 12 both connect OSPF to RIP 2. Router 13 advertises network 59 from RIP 1 into OSPF. If routers 11 and 12 advertise routes to network 59 into RIP 2 with different costs, routing information may travel back and forth between these two routers as they share both the original and the translated information. Try to avoid redistribution; routers in this scenario should be configured as border routers.

Redistribution

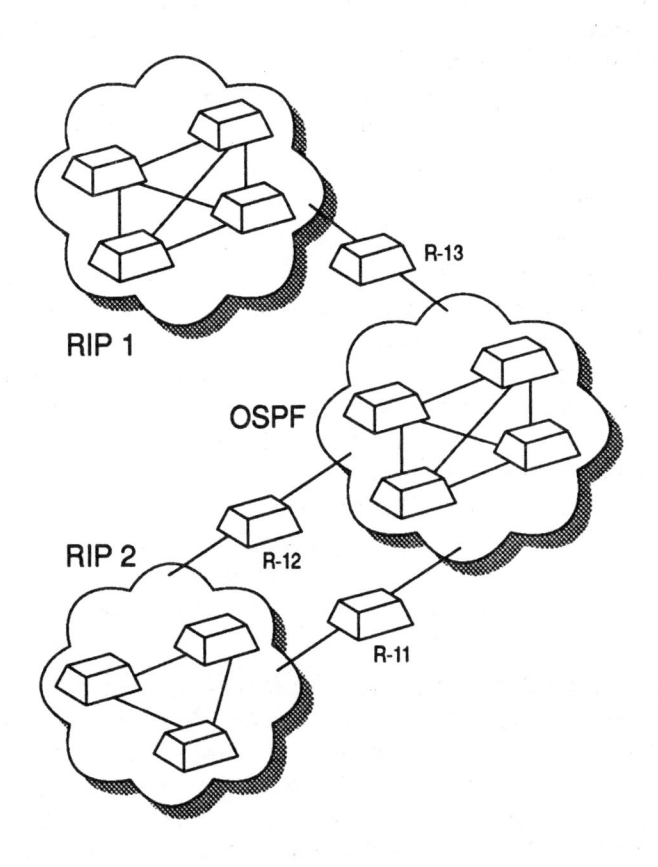

Ships in the Night vs. Integrated Routing

The two basic approaches to multiple routing protocols running on the same router are known as **Ships in the Night** (SIN) and **integrated routing**. SIN was discussed in *Mastering Internetworking*: each protocol creates and maintains its own routing database and ignores the existence of other protocols, much as unrelated merchant shipping in a busy port will ignore each other except to avoid collisions. Integrated routing requires the protocols to contribute information to each other and create an integrated database.

SIN has the advantage in the market today because it makes it easy to add another protocol onto the router or upgrade protocols without affecting other protocols. Since each protocol considers itself alone in the universe, your router, instead of sending out one routing table update every 90 seconds (as it would in the IPX version of RIP), will send out several updates: IPX/RIP every 90 seconds, RTMP every 10 seconds, standard RIP every 60 seconds, and IGRP every 60 seconds. Can you imagine how much bandwidth you're wasting?! Then there's what I call the "Mother always loved you better" syndrome that you get caught up in when your Novell users end up with significantly better response time than your XNS users, or vice versa. It's hard to explain to end users that SIN puts them in different logical routed networks from their neighbors.

Advantages of integrated routing include much less bandwidth wasted by updates and possibly faster convergence if link state information is shared with distance vector protocols. Suppose you have a router combining OSPF and RIP when OSPF receives a link update saying network 42 has become unreachable. With SIN, RIP will continue trying to reach network 42 until it decides that 42 is unreachable. With integrated routing, the integrated database will learn that network 42 is unreachable as soon as OSPF discovers it. Integrated IS/IS integrates routing information from RIP and IS/IS so it's popular in networks running both TCP/IP and OSI stacks.

ADVANCED ROUTING

SIN

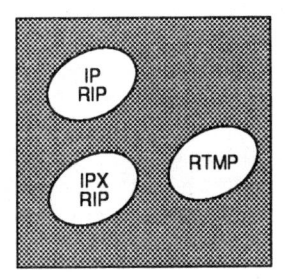

- Each Protocol upgrades separately
- Problems occur separately
- Users exist in separate virtual networks

Integrated Routing

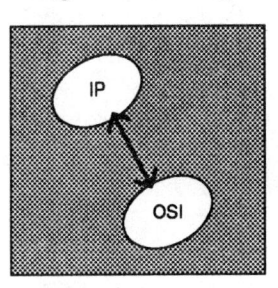

- Databases integrated
- Protocols share advantages
- Protocols share failures, problems

Routing Unroutable Traffic

NetBIOS and LAT, as well as other protocols, can't be routed because they don't have a Network Layer. Routers look for a network address. One solution, of course, is to put an IP header on the packet. Another emerging solution is to arrange for the router to learn the Data Link location of local user devices and then create a route to the destination while bypassing the Network Layer. Vendors have been active in developing software that will create address tables of end users based on their Ethernet addresses.

Local Area Transport (**LAT**) is a DEC terminal emulation protocol that does not include a Network Layer. If you are using bridges for your LAT traffic you can create a tunnel between two specific bridges and have only these bridges connect LAT traffic. The Maintenance Operation Protocol (MOP), also unroutable, gives you quick maintenance and downloading of protocols.

Being able to "route" SNA traffic across another protocol backbone is high on your wish list if you are working to eliminate parallel networks. We will discuss this in detail in Chapter 6. SNA is frequently referred to as unroutable because it does not have a network layer that routers can recognize. SNA traffic is routed by **Type 5** host **nodes** and **Type 4** Communication Controller **nodes** in what are known as **subareas**. Type 5 and Type 4 nodes are known as subarea nodes because they define a subarea. The subarea nodes perform **intermediate routing services** so they use SNA's Path Control Layer information to create routes from sender to receiver. In Chapter 6, we will discuss IBM's APPN routing for peer-to-peer networks. Some vendors are suggesting that network managers replace their Type 4 nodes in SNA subareas with multi-protocol routers. Usually this is part of a strategy in which you are merging an SNA backbone with an existing IP backbone. Type 4 nodes have Network Control Program (**NCP**) software running and use static routing tables, a big difference from how routers work, generating dynamic routing tables.

Unroutable – Mostly

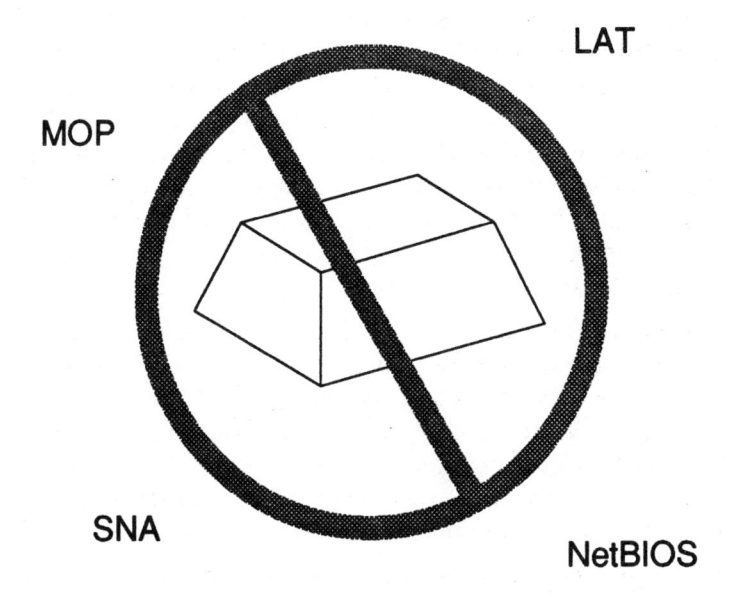

MOP

LAT

SNA

NetBIOS

Wide-Area Routing

Because wide-area links run at lower speeds compared to LAN, remote bridges and routers need to find ways to avoid wasting bandwidth. Group addressing schemes, if your router software includes one, can drop your WAN utilization significantly: instead of sending multiple packets over your WAN link, you send one packet with a multicast address. The receiving router either makes multiple copies for each receiver or simply forwards the multicast address, depending on what the end user software understands. Using source route bridging over WAN links creates incredible bottlenecks, so if you find yourself in this situation, question your vendor closely on multicast addressing and/or SR disablement on WAN links. NetBIOS networks seem to develop broadcast storms quite readily so be sure you investigate your vendor's claims in this area.

Dialup (async) **routers**, with integrated modems, provide good solutions for scattered offices that produce low traffic volume. When it gets a connection request to a remote network, the router dials a temporary connection, sends the packet(s) and then terminates the connection. These dialup routers can give you considerable cost savings in locations that do not generate enough traffic to justify a leased line. A dialup router coupled with wireless networks is discussed in Chapter 6.

Data compression can significantly lower your WAN phone bill. A 14.4 Kbps modem can achieve up to 56 Kbps of throughput, using compression. You can also investigate load balancing between multiple routers or between multiple ports on the same router. In the local network environment, user devices send their routing requests to one router and only use alternate routers after a redirect from the primary router. You could use dynamic load balancing to improve performance on your WAN links. Burst Mode IPX can significantly boost performance in Novell networks by allowing a stream of packets to pass without requiring individual acknowledgments. Finally, timeouts can create a significant WAN performance problem, especially in SNA networks running on IP routers. We will discuss this in Chapter 6.

WAN Strategies

- Multicast
- Disable SR explorers
- NetBIOS disablement
- Data compression
- Load balancing
- Burst mode
- Dialup routers

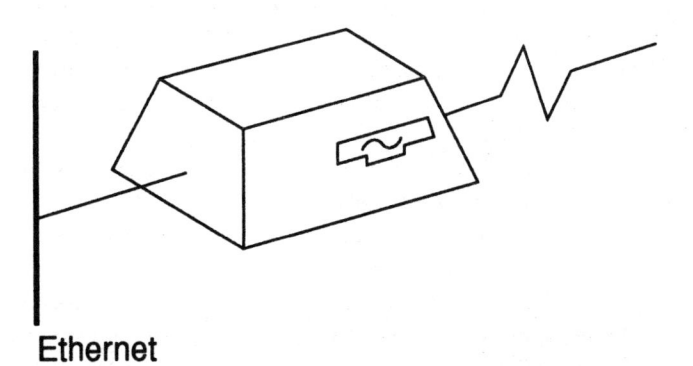

Ethernet

The Future of Routing

Earlier concepts about the differences between bridges and routers are disappearing as router speed equals wire speed and the need for router functionality moves out into more and more networks. Routing integration with the wiring infrastructure (hubs) is sure to accelerate as the 90s progress. This puts your internet infrastructure into your wiring infrastructure. Connecting several networks to an integrated bridge/router moves some local internet traffic across the local backbone of the router backplane. If the router connects these networks to a core backbone, this core will see less traffic. This improves performance for the entire company.

Most of this chapter has focused on IP, but other protocols are also enhancing their routing functions. It would be an understatement to say that AppleTalk was not designed for multi-protocol internetworking using complex topologies and multiple levels of routers. AppleTalk's routing protocol, called the Routing Table Maintenance Protocol (**RTMP**), uses distance vectors like RIP does but has problems with performance over WANs and complex internets because it was designed for small networks. *Every 10 seconds*, an RTMP router broadcasts its routing information database. A new inter-domain protocol called **AURP** will broadcast only when changes occur, but it's designed for point to point links. AppleTalk will eventually be extended to include OSPF and/or IS/IS. AURP also specifies how to encapsulate AppleTalk into TCP/IP.

Novell has a new link state protocol called the IPX Link State Routing Protocol (ILSR). The IETF is considering IS/IS for use in the Internet, along with OSPF and Integrated IS/IS. Integrated IS/IS is popular in networks that run TCP/IP as well as OSI protocols. Chapter 6 brings you details on some architectures that use these protocols for multi-platform distributed computing.

AURP –
Saving Bandwidth in AppleTalk Networks

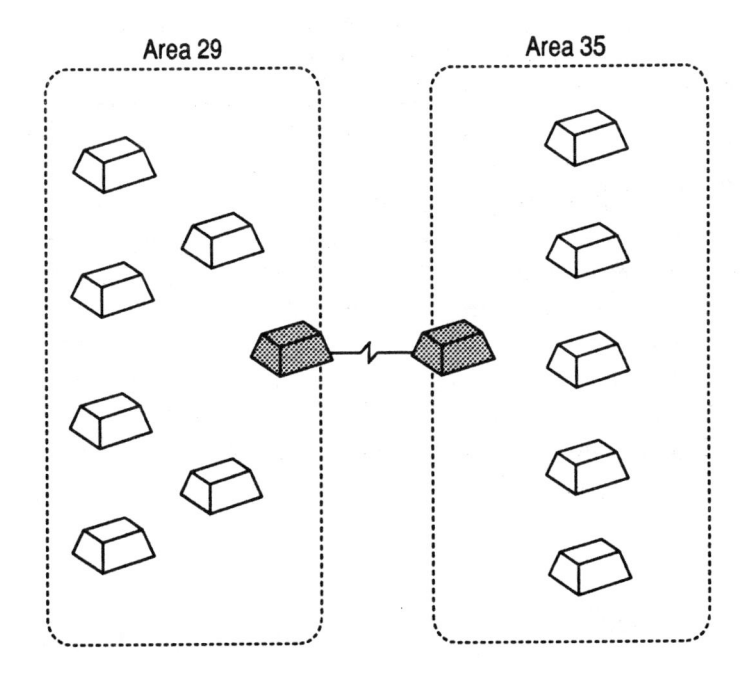

- Only when changes occur
- Point-to-point links only

Summary

- Link state routing protocols like OSPF and IS/IS converge on a new network topology faster than distance vector protocols like RIP.
- Subnetworking gives your network a hierarchical routing flow that makes your network more manageable.
- The new BGP protocol allows separate areas to connect with each other without traversing the core backbone, speeding response time through the internet.
- Redistributing routing information between routers using different routing protocols should be done carefully to avoid routing loops.
- The two approaches to multiple protocols running on the same router are called Ships In The Night (SIN) and Integrated Routing.
- Routers can handle "unroutable" protocols like SNA and LAT by creating tunnels, by encapsulating or by using proprietary routing schemes.
- Dialup routers provide good solutions for scattered offices with relatively light traffic.

Review – Chapter 3

1. Draw a line between statements on the left and acronyms on the right.

    A. OSI link state standard   a. BGP
    B. New standard for inter-domain   b. IS/IS
    C. Link state standard (Internet)   c. EGP
    D. Popular distance vector standard   d. RIP
    E. Old border router protocol   e. OSPF
    F. Cisco owns it   f. IDRP
    G. New OSI border protocol   g. IGRP

2. What are the major advantages of link state protocols over distance vector protocols?
3. What does EGP stand for?
4. Do NOSs communicate with level 2 routers? When would they do this?
5. What does BGP stand for?
6. Are you planning to use EGP in your network? What criteria will you use to decide?
7. Assume that you have a network that is using the RIP protocol, and your company acquires a smaller company which will now become a subsidiary. This new company has routers that can only use IS/IS. Will you decide to use one protocol or will you continue to use both routing protocols? Why or why not? What are the trade-offs?
8. If a border router fails, what will happen in your internet?
9. In OSPF, when are link state updates sent out?
10. If a router's port A fails, will it still send out routing updates on that port? On other ports?
11. If link A fails, what will port A (attached to it) do?
12. How many network addresses does an integrated bridge/router have in an IP network?
13. What criteria would you use to create independent domains in your network?

14. What is Apple's new routing protocol called?
15. What is the major advantage of Apple's new protocol?
16. What routing protocol do you think most Novell networks use today?
17. Your integrated bridge/router has SR and SRT bridging and can do SNA, IP and IPX routing as well as SDLC passthrough. Can you use this device to connect token ring to an SNA/SDLC network? (Can it translate SDLC to 802.2 LLC?)
18. Does holddown speed up convergence? Why or why not?
19. OSPF routers share _____ states with each other.
20. The path from a router to its designated router is an _____.
21. A collection of networks is an area, _____ or _____. A collection of IDRP areas is a _____.
22. Link state protocols use _____ and _____ to make sure LSPs are new LSPs.
23. Can you use Integrated IS/IS to run the network in question #17?
24. List one advantage of SIN. List one disadvantage.
25. Subarea routing depends on type __ and type __ nodes, _____ and _____ respectively.
26. Scattered offices with low traffic volume can use _____ routers.
27. What is the maximum number of hosts you can attach to a class C IP network?

ADVANCED ROUTING 73

Key Words

The words and phrases highlighted in **bold** represent key concepts in this chapter. Please take the time now to write down your own definitions of these terms, using the list below and additional paper if needed. Then compare your efforts to the training text. This is an excellent way for you to determine weak points in the breadth and depth of your understanding of this chapter.

slow convergence

OSPF

IS/IS

distance vector

counting to infinity

unreachable

holddown

split horizon

link state

link state flooding

neighbor discovery

advertisements

topology map

HELLO

neighbors

areas

domains

autonomous systems

designated router

adjacency

neighbor greeting

ADVANCED ROUTING

- LSP
- LSA
- time stamp
- sequence numbers
- subnetworking
- local routers
- level 1 routers
- border routers
- level 2 routers
- intra-domain routing
- inter-domain routing
- internal router
- external
- inter-AS
- EGP
- core
- BGP
- IDRP
- BIS
- confederation
- classes of address
- network ID
- host ID
- Network Entity Title
- Network Service Access Points
- redistribution
- redistribution loops
- Ships In The Night
- integrated routing
- LAT
- Type 5 nodes
- Type 4 nodes
- subareas
- intermediate routing services
- NCP
- dialup routers
- RTMP
- AURP

4
Network Operating Systems & Middleware

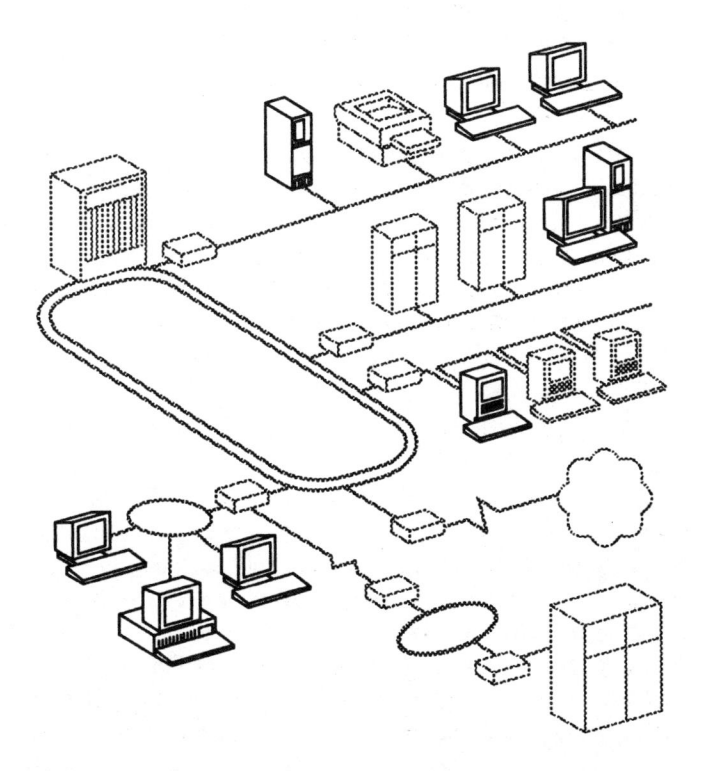

Goals of this Chapter

When you complete this chapter, you will have reviewed:
- ☐ List the advantages and disadvantages of 4 major network operating systems (NOSs) and how they interoperate
- ☐ List the business benefits of client/server computing
- ☐ List 2 desktop operating systems used as NOSs
- ☐ Define middleware and its role in network Session Layer operations

Servers, Network Operating Systems and Middleware

The earliest servers were software slapped onto the cheapest hardware platform available, designed for printer sharing and generally not even dedicated to that task. The dedicated PC-based server was a step up from this basic level of service. Today's high-performance servers are dedicated platforms with workstation or minicomputer engines, giving network managers more MIPs, faster RISC (reduced instruction set computing) processing, multitasking and multiprocessing operations and greater reliability.

The software entities that manage server operations are called **network operating systems** (NOSs). In the same way that a device operating system manages the interface between a device's I/O and memory management functions and its user applications, the NOS manages the interface between the network's underlying transport capabilities and the applications resident on servers. NOS software resides at the equivalent of the OSI Model's Session and Presentation Layers, with a little bit of Application Layer functions thrown in.

The NOS can be considered part of middleware, the software layer that resides between the transport infrastructure and the application. Application developers can write their code to a middleware application program interface (API) instead of needing multiple hooks to accommodate all the available network types, speeding application development. A multi-NOS world is a diverse software environment in which application developers need middleware more each day. Vendors who develop middleware are moving us closer to the day when the network can be considered one single computing entity, with specific tasks distributed transparently throughout the network "computer."

In this chapter, we will study the NetWare, LAN Manager, VINES and LAN Server NOSs in detail, and briefly mention UNIX, AppleShare, and System 7. We will end with interoperability and future evolutionary trends. After looking at NOSs, we will survey middleware needs in large networks. All the software discussed in this chapter provides Session Layer services for networks, either as NOSs or more broadly as middleware.

Network Operating Systems

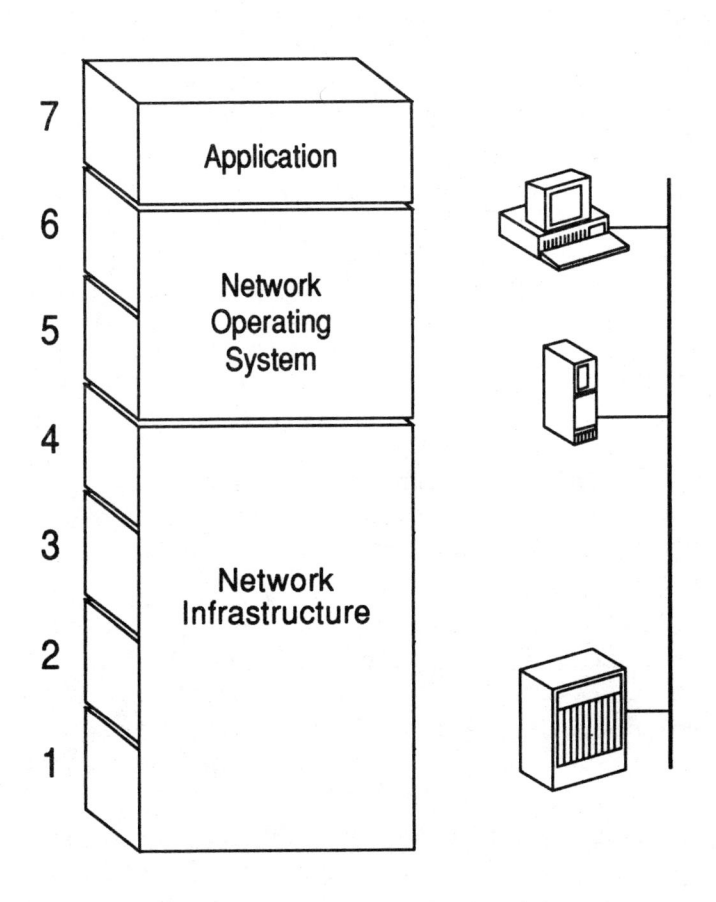

Rise of Client/Server Computing

The next step in server evolution—the **client/server computing** model—carries the server to its logical role as the primary focus of information dispersal in the network. Users in a client/server computing environment can access information stored anywhere in the internet, providing an entirely new information infrastructure.

In the client/server computing model, the server and its clients share the computing role between them. The server performs database access and intensive computing tasks (the back end processes) and the client performs the display and user-interface of the results of those calculations (the front end processes). In a standard server model, the server receives a database request and transports a copy of the entire database to the requestor. This clogs the network and compromises security. In the client/server computing model, only results are transmitted, conserving network bandwidth. Each component can be developed, migrated and serviced separately. Components are developed to optimize a particular function, either database retrieval or information display. Existing resources are leveraged with lower cost platforms (compared to mainframes and FEPs) and a preserved investment in hardware, software and training.

The client/server computing model helps bring essentially flat networks into a more hierarchical framework for easier and more effective management. As networks grow in size, segmenting managed resources into logical management domains allows managers to automate some tasks, zero in on problem areas faster and spend time analyzing and planning rather than just fire-fighting.

When you implement a NOS in your network, both end users and servers have software installed: a smaller agent for end users and a full implementation on the server. You can buy software to automate the end user installation. You don't need to buy software that implements client/server computing in order to use a NOS.

Client/Server Computing

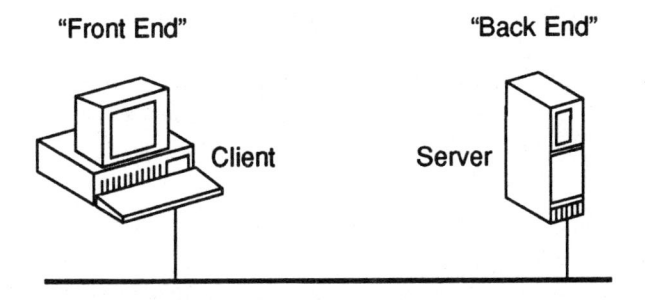

"Front End" "Back End"

Client Server

- Generate Requests
- Display results

- Database Storage & Retrieval
- Processing

NOS Market Survey

The total value of the NOS market was about $800 million in 1992, and is growing rapidly. **NetWare** by Novell holds about 65% of the market. IBM's NOS, **LAN Server**, holds about 5%, approximately 2% less than Banyan **VINES**. **LAN Manager** owns about 3% of the market. Macintosh users in an AppleTalk network of fewer than ten nodes can use a Mac with **System 7** as a server but with 10–100 nodes, **AppleShare** is a better choice. In multi-desktop networks, Macintosh users frequently access other servers using NetWare or VINES. Artisoft's LANtastic has about 15% of the market for small networks specifically. DEC's Pathworks, which is based on LAN Manager, has about 5% of the market. UNIX, if its installations as a server NOS are counted, holds about 6% of the NOS market.

As you make your NOS choice, keep your five-year future growth needs in mind. Small networks need low cost and low memory requirements while large networks need powerful distributed management, global naming and a robust directory service. **Global naming** means that users have access to all network resources by name, without having to know the resource's physical location. It also means that users can log into any local server and get access to the resources they need, because their user profiles (including access rights) are globally known. Having resources accessible by name, and not requiring their physical location to be specified, makes a NOS network-based, rather than server-based. This movement toward non-hardware-dependent access forms the basis for true distributed computing. The CCITT/ISO **X.500** Directory Service standard is an example of a global **directory** of name/location mapping, essentially a "white pages" for network users.

Without global naming, users log on to an individual server, so network managers must create scripts to log a particular user onto more than one server at a time. If the user or the server moves or if the access rights to any server or service changes, every script must be changed. With more than 1,000 users, you definitely need global naming and a directory.

The NOS Market

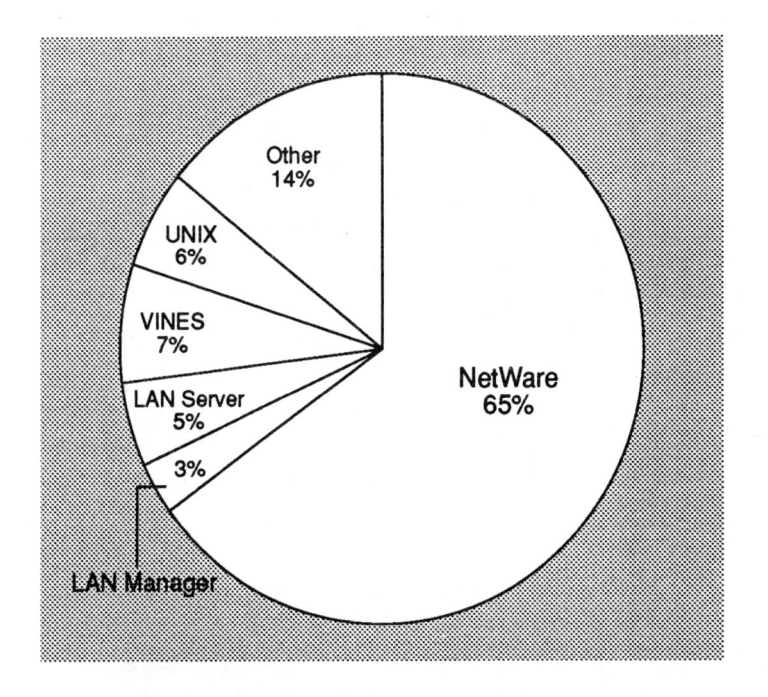

- NetWare 65%
- Other 14%
- UNIX 6%
- VINES 7%
- LAN Server 5%
- LAN Manager 3%

NetWare

NetWare was originally designed to serve small PC LANs and it shows. Its Extended File Salvage means a server only actually recovers the space allocated to "deleted" user files when it runs out of free space. Thus, users with second thoughts may be able to get their discarded files back if the server's memory is not heavily loaded.

Because of its 65% market share, many network managers find themselves choosing NetWare more because they have to coexist with an existing network than because of any feature list. Nevertheless, NetWare 4.0 includes important new features that are well worth looking at, especially new X.400 electronic mail and TP4 support and a simple directory service. The new global naming software moves NetWare 4.0 away from server-specific resource binding, a long overdue move. Networks with 100 nodes or less frequently choose **NetWare Lite**.

NetWare has versions for most desktops and expects to eventually run over most transport protocols. You can implement NetWare for Ethernet, Token Ring, LocalTalk and ARCnet. Most other NOSs contain agents to link them to NetWare in multi-NOS networks.

NetWare for SAA, a new gateway product, runs as a NetWare Loadable Module (**NLM**)—a fancy term for "application". This NLM runs in a NetWare file server and allows NetWare clients to connect to two hosts through FEPs using the same gateway. Putting the software on an existing server saves money compared to dedicated gateway hardware.

The latest versions of the four major NOSs discussed in this chapter will give you most of these high performance features:

- High performance filing system
- Fault tolerance: hot fixes and **disk mirroring** (every bit on the disk is "mirrored" on a second disk, so that disk failure will not affect performance)
- Central Administration
- Support for multiple user desktops, transport protocols and server engines.
- **Multitasking** and **multiprocessing**, 32 bit operation.

NetWare Evolution

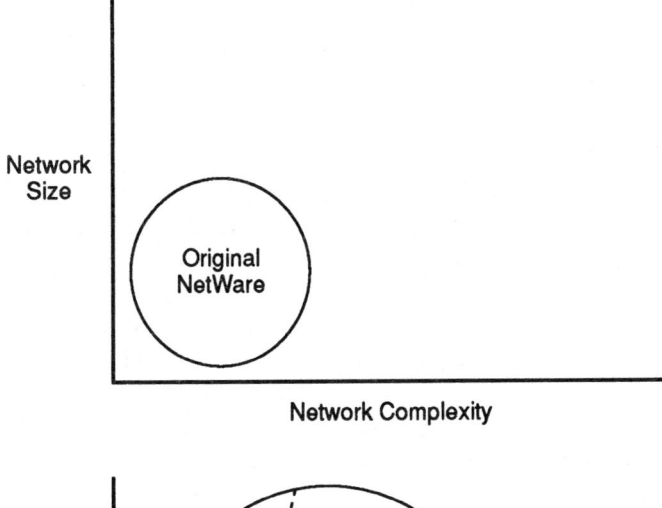

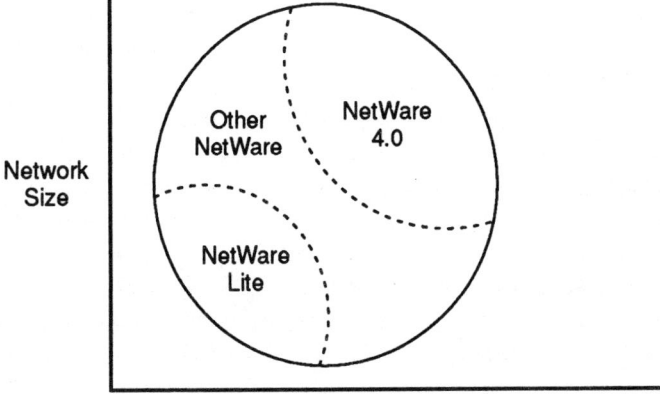

Network Size vs *Network Complexity*: Original NetWare

Network Size vs *Network Complexity*: Other NetWare, NetWare 4.0, NetWare Lite

VINES

VINES performs especially well in networks with large numbers of users, servers and traffic because it is particularly easy for network managers to add, delete and move users and server offerings. One of the great selling points of VINES is **StreetTalk**, its global naming service. Building systems with 5,000 users and 100 servers is much easier to manage if you can mount new software using global commands rather than having to upgrade every one of those 100 servers individually. Networks should consider VINES if they are very large, have extensive WAN connections or need OSI or another "open systems" design.

The newest version of VINES (5.0) features greater integration of services, better WAN connectivity, greater portability to all versions of UNIX, a new filing system and better Macintosh support. You can purchase an optional SNMP agent and manage the network remotely via X.25 connections. Existing UNIX servers can become VINES servers by purchasing a special service pack rather than the full NOS implementation. VINES 5.0 supports clients using DOS, Windows, OS/2, UNIX and Macintosh computers. Mac users can tunnel using VINES IP. (Essentially, two AppleTalk networks connect at the Session Layer using VINES and at the Network Layer using IP, bypassing bridging). You can also allow Mac users to exchange e-mail with non-Mac users via VINES.

Banyan has modified VINES to support LAN Manager protocols and APIs, allowing its NOS to support mail, print, filing and other LAN Manager APIs, as well as NP. VINES StreetTalk can provide network management information on both VINES and LAN Manager nodes. Banyan and Microsoft are swapping technical specifications for the NOS code so they can build future applications that will run on both NOSs. VINES APIs also allow NetWare servers to be managed through VINES. The new Enterprise Services for NetWare can be loaded on NetWare servers to give them StreetTalk and other advanced VINES services without trashing the existing software. Enterprise Services includes an NLM for the NetWare servers, APIs for work stations and an Enterprise server to support the NetWare servers.

VINES

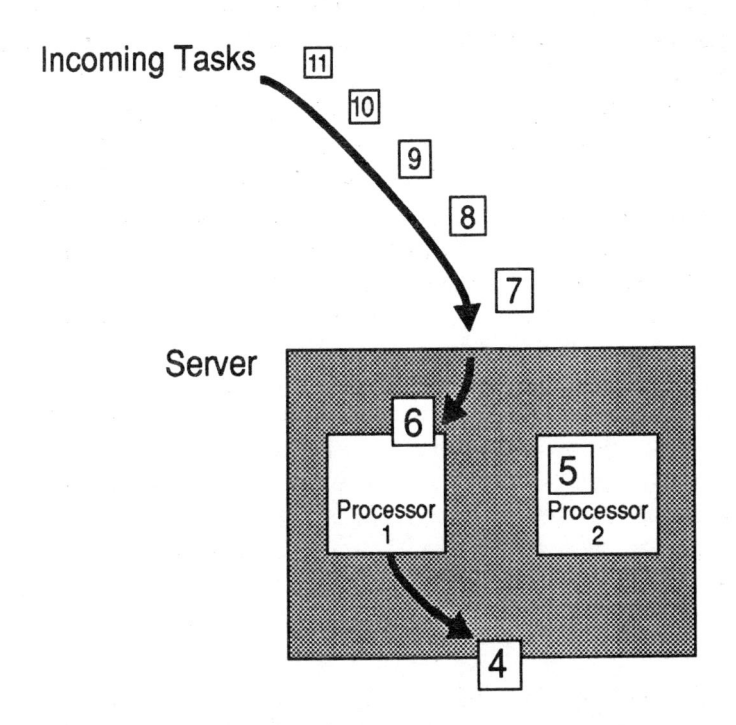

Incoming Tasks

Server

Processor 1

Processor 2

VINES 5.0 Features:
- VINES File Store, which allows file servers to support file objects for a wide variety of client operating systems
- Symmetrical multiprocessing, which means that different tasks can be assigned to separate processors within the server
- Directory synchronization, which keeps distributed directories updated
- Better print services, including allowing users to schedule print jobs, and the creation of a status midway between a user and a LAN administrator, so that these individuals can play with print queues but cannot wreak any broader havoc. The administrator can set multiple printers for a queue and multiple queues for a printer. Users always know where their job is printing

LAN Manager

LAN Manager began as a joint 3Com/Microsoft project, which Microsoft now owns. Version 2.2 includes support for Macintosh desktops as well as DOS, Windows, UNIX and OS/2. Servers can use UNIX, OS/2, Windows NT and VMS engines and will support users on Ethernet, Token Ring and Arcnet, using TCP/IP, NetBEUI, SPP/IDP and OSI TP4. LAN Manager 2.2 includes NetView and SNMP agents.

LAN Manager's more interesting features include the domain concept (don't confuse this with OSI's domain discussed in Chapter 3), **Named Pipes** (NP) and both multitasking and multiprocessing operations. A network manager sets up a logical domain of servers and can apply commands to them as a group; this automates many tedious network operations, including moves, adds and deletes of users, applications and security authorizations. Multiprocessing operations put multiple processors to work within one server. In **symmetrical multiprocessing** (as in VINES), the processors share the load equally; the **asymmetrical** form dedicates each processor for certain tasks so they cannot load-share dynamically. In LAN Manager, one processor will be devoted to a certain set of operations—disk I/O, for example—and all disk read/write requests will be automatically routed to that processor, leaving the second processor free for other work.

A pipe is a Presentation Layer entity that allows process–process communication; it is created for a specific communication and disappears when the communication is complete. A Named Pipe is a permanent logical structure that gives you the opportunity to re-direct interprocess communication without multiple NetBIOS calls. Once an NP is listed in a server directory as a shared resource, anyone can access it. NPs give developers a simple, generic high-level interface for their API development. **Peer services** are becoming more important in segmented, workstation-oriented networks where a workstation can act as a non-dedicated server to peers for a single low-level function—fetching mail, perhaps—while still acting as a standalone device for its end user.

Windows 2.2 at the server was designed to complement Windows For Workgroups at the workstation and is tightly integrated with Windows NT. New WAN features include Remote Access Services 1.1 which allows remote users to dialin to X.25 networks. On the Windows front, the network administrator can manage multiple servers, including remotely.

LAN Manager

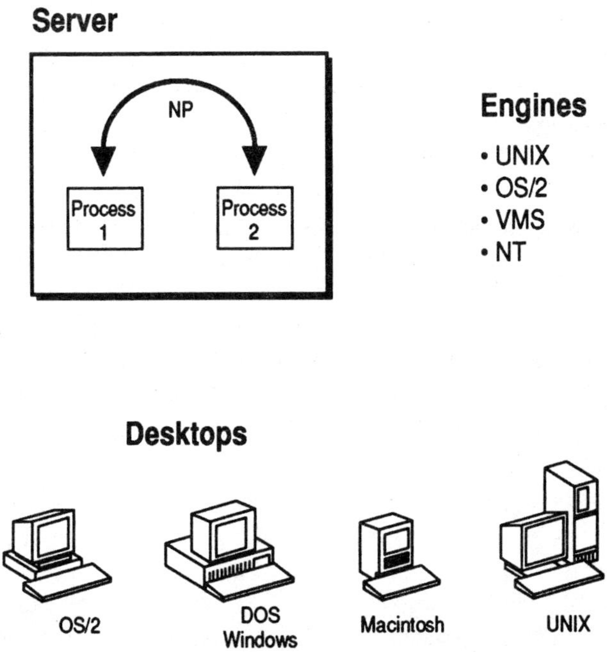

Server

NP
Process 1 → Process 2

Engines
- UNIX
- OS/2
- VMS
- NT

Desktops

OS/2   DOS Windows   Macintosh   UNIX

LAN Server and Device OSs

LAN Manager spawned IBM's LAN Server but the two NOSs took different development roads and today are not very interoperable. LAN Server 3.0 runs on OS/2 2.0 and is the first 32 bit version of this NOS. The 3.0 release can handle 1,000 clients per server and uses asymmetrical multiprocessing. LAN Server networks can support multiple network transport protocols and VINES, NetWare, LAN Manager and LANtastic servers using IBM's Network Transport Services/2 (**NTS/2**). LAN Server for Macintosh 1.0 software lets DOS, Windows, OS/2 and Mac users share server files. IBM says that LAN Server will evolve towards support for the Open Software Foundation's (OSF) Distributed Computing Environment (DCE) standard. IBM also offers NetWare for Token Ring networks that need non-IBM interoperability. LAN Server passes network management information to NetView and LAN Network Manager, IBM's two management products. Configuration, Installation and Distribution (CID) allows remote software distribution, a plus for large networks.

While NOSs have been evolving, device operating systems—particularly **UNIX**—have moved beyond the desktop to become a formidable force in certain network environments. UNIX, with its 32 bit data handling and extensive communications utilities, has been evolving from a desktop OS to an almost-NOS for a decade. Now that interoperability of UNIX versions is becoming more the norm, and major desktop vendors like Apple, IBM, Hewlett-Packard and others sell UNIX derivatives, UNIX is well placed to contend as a NOS in small single-NOS networks and to communicate with other NOSs in multi-NOS networks. VINES has been most aggressive about UNIX links but NetWare and LAN Manager are not far behind. (LAN Manager for UNIX is an example of such products.) The percentage of NetWare servers linked to UNIX should climb to between 25% and 35% of all NetWare servers by the mid-decade. **Windows NT** is another example of software that started as a desktop OS and is evolving into network software. A convergence of function is inevitable as the manufacturers of user devices and operating systems push the envelope of their products' capabilities.

Now that we've surveyed the NOSs, let's work on some cases.

A Multi-NOS Network

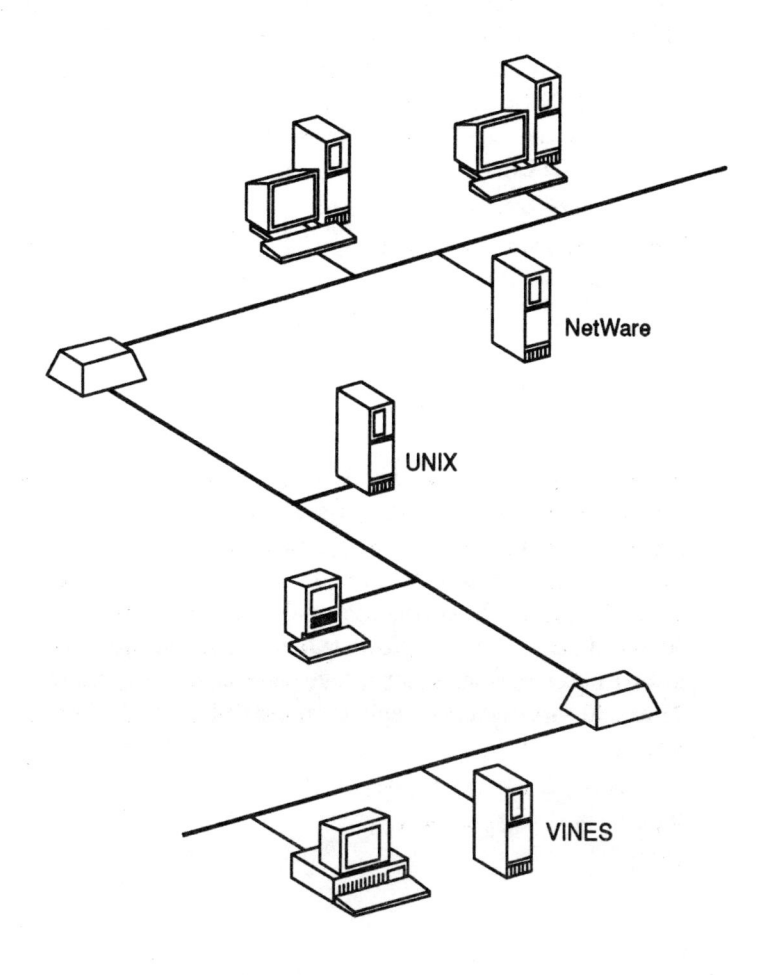

Each segment of this network has a server offering a different NOS but users have access to all the information because NOSs include each others' agents.

Choosing A NOS

☐ The Super Healthy Ice Cream Company has 125 small branch offices in the Seattle area, with only one or two computers each. Most offices use Windows but two insist on Macintoshes. The main data center has VAX and Tandem mainframes, nine Ethernets, an FDDI backbone, and has two additional Ethernets dedicated to 12 servers. The nine Ethernets support 625 desktops, which include DOS, Windows, UNIX and Mac users.

What network services do you need?

What NOS(s) will you choose?

WHY?

☐ The Heavy Rocks Construction Company of Little Rock does a thriving multi-state business in gravel and other highway construction materials. Seventy nine network management staffers support the main data center with IBM and DEC mainframes, 21 Token Rings (plus three backbones) and desktops with DOS, Windows and OS/2. They are migrating from mainframe applications to a client/server architecture and are planning to install between 25 and 30 superservers to replace various FEPs and older mainframes.

What network services do you need?

What NOS(s) will you choose?

WHY?

WAN & Data Center

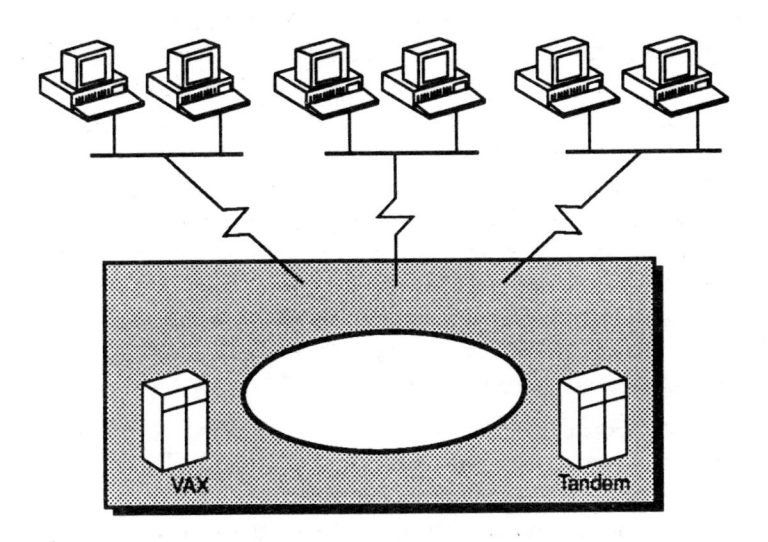

Downsizing & Token Ring

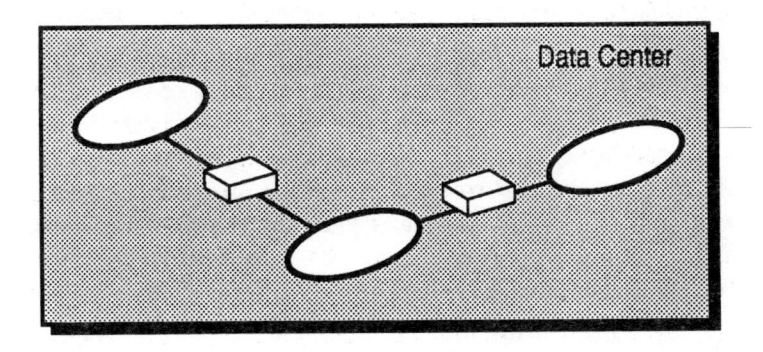

Middleware

NOS vendors don't like to admit it but the fact is that except for very small networks, you need more than just a NOS. What you need is **middleware**, the software layer at approximately OSI's Session Layer that separates network transport from applications. Application developers today have to deal directly with multiple transport platforms and multiple transport protocols, which means application developers spend too much energy dealing with the complexities of communications protocols and end users don't have transparent access to corporate information. Middleware gives developers a single "mega-API" to work with and shields them from transport details. As network software at the lower layers becomes more complex and diverse, application developers need more powerful middleware.

IBM is developing Message Queue Manager (**MQM**) for high volume transaction processing via messaging. Another product called Datatrade has extensive repository and distributed services. A repository maintains relationships between objects, such as domains, applications, services and users. When a request is received, the repository knows which services are available to which users. If the local server can't accommodate the request, it is routed to another server that can. Many needs—security, for instance—are global and should be handled by middleware rather than by individual protocols or applications.

Middleware comes in four types: distributed filing, distributed database (**SQL**), distributed messaging, and distributed procedures (**RPC**). You can classify remote procedure calls (RPCs) and structured query languages (SQLs) as middleware because they let you move data without worrying about network protocols. Third-party vendors offer a wide array of ever more powerful middleware products. In addition, middleware also encompasses LU 6.2, NP, Sockets and other transport or NOS-specific protocols.

The UNIX approach to middleware centers on interprocess communications (**IPCs**) like shared memory and pipes to coordinate and integrate communication between processes within a machine. Some vendors are working on IPCs that will allow UNIX versions and look-alikes, as well as Windows and OS/2 machines, to communicate.

Middleware

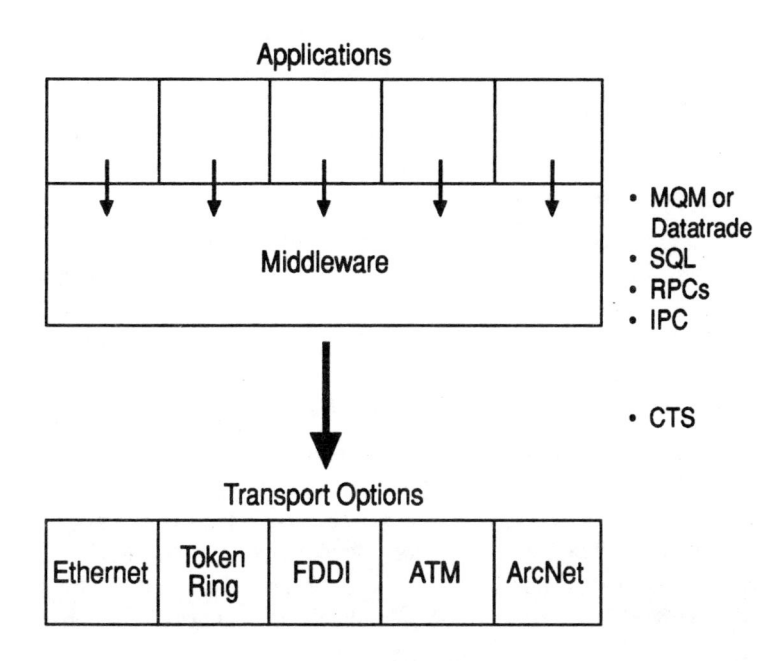

```
                    Applications
    ┌─────┬─────┬─────┬─────┬─────┐
    │     │     │     │     │     │
    │  ↓  │  ↓  │  ↓  │  ↓  │  ↓  │
    ├─────┴─────┴─────┴─────┴─────┤      • MQM or
    │                             │        Datatrade
    │         Middleware          │      • SQL
    │                             │      • RPCs
    └─────────────┬───────────────┘      • IPC
                  │
                  ↓                      • CTS
              Transport Options
    ┌────────┬──────┬──────┬─────┬────────┐
    │Ethernet│Token │ FDDI │ ATM │ ArcNet │
    │        │ Ring │      │     │        │
    └────────┴──────┴──────┴─────┴────────┘
```

The Evolution of NOSs and Middleware

The NOS began simply as a server-enabler in small, PC-based LANs but has evolved into a network management tool, an enabler of other software, a platform for user interfaces and network-wide presentation standards and an integral cornerstone of middleware.

NOSs must be able to deliver applications to all users regardless of their device operating systems and transport protocols and most NOSs do, to some extent. The more multi-technology your network is, the more protocol-independence you need in your NOS. As mergers, acquisitions, joint ventures and similar business activities increase in the 1990s, networks must accommodate these changes.

NetWare and UNIX are the prime contenders for industry standards, but users need to be able to access information on servers that may be running different NOSs, so NOSs must be able to freely interoperate. In addition, every NOS must be able to send standard management information to a management console that can communicate via SNMP or other standard.

The NOS must ultimately fit into a client/server computing architecture that embraces more and more sophisticated user devices. Client/server computing and accompanying powerful NOSs will redesign every concept of information management the average corporation now holds. In order to accomplish this, future NOSs need symmetrical multiprocessing platforms based on 32 or 64 bit multi-tasking pathways, peer processing, multi-protocol transport interfaces, extensive APIs and extensive security features.

Most importantly, middleware must continue to evolve in its role as the universal underpinning for application development. Middleware offers application developers the tools that they need not only to streamline application development but also to move applications farther away from today's dependence on the network technology and transport software. Until we have true transparency of this kind, developers will not be able to give end users the distributed applications and the distributed computing power that they need and want.

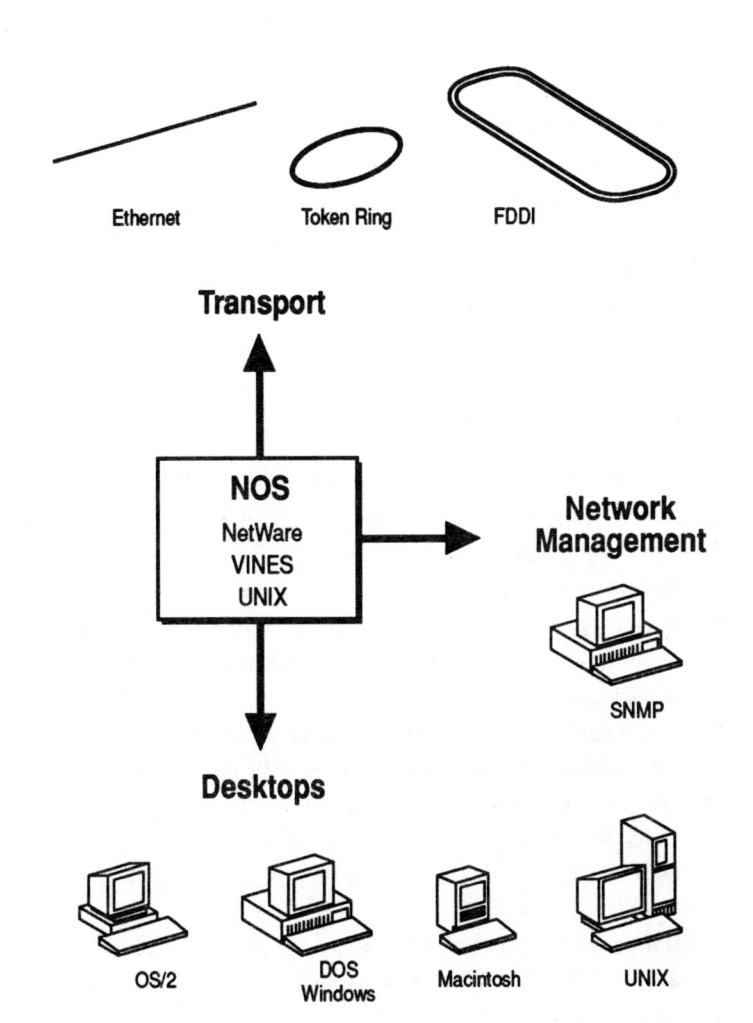

The Evolution of NOSs

Ethernet Token Ring FDDI

Transport

NOS
NetWare
VINES
UNIX

Network Management

SNMP

Desktops

OS/2 DOS Windows Macintosh UNIX

Summary

- A network operating system (NOS) manages the interface between the network's transport and applications.
- The most important NOSs are NetWare, VINES, LAN Manager and LAN Server.
- Device operating systems, most notably UNIX, are evolving network functions rivaling that of a NOS.
- NOSs, along with RPCs and IPCs, form middleware. Middleware APIs simplify application development by making underlying transport details irrelevant.
- Interoperability is the key to NOS future evolution.

Review – Chapter 4

1. At what layer(s) of the OSI model do NOSs operate?
2. List three of the four most popular NOSs in use in the U.S. today.
3. Which NOS has the largest market share?
4. Why does this NOS have such a large market share?
5. If you have a small (less than fifty node) network of relatively homogeneous devices, which NOS is probably best suited for your needs? Why?
6. If you have a large internetwork with heterogeneous device types and multiple network protocols in use (i.e. a multi-vendor network environment), which network operating system is probably best suited to your needs?
7. How are the various NOSs evolving to interoperate with each other?
8. If my network is using NetWare and your network is using VINES, are we doomed to eternal non-interoperability? Why or why not?
9. NOSs need to be transport - _____.
10. A software element that sits on a NetWare server and allows a VINES manager to manage that NetWare server is called a VINES _____.
11. The two main computing models in use today are the mainframe

NETWORK OPERATING SYSTEMS & MIDDLEWARE

model and the _____ computing model.

12. What are some of the specific business advantages of the second model?
13. In a client/server network the server does the _____ tasks while the end user display device does the _____ tasks.
14. The IBM network operating system is known as _____.
15. Network operating systems evolved as a way to help network managers control (device) operation.
16. Name 2 advantages of NetWare compared to VINES. Name 2 advantages of VINES compared to NetWare.
17. The most important desktop operating system that has evolved to become a NOS is _____.
18. Which other NOSs are based on the desktop OS you listed in #17?
19. What kind of multiprocessing does LAN Manager use? (The text doesn't say. You have to figure it out.)
20. What is middleware and what is its role in network operations?
21. For each term listed below, indicate whether you consider it part of middleware:
    Ethernet
    FDDI
    APPN
    NetWare
    Excel
    NP
    SQL
    Datatrade
    Most client/server applications
22. Does a network with 25 nodes need middleware? Why or why not?
23. What about a network with 250 nodes? If your answer change, why?

Key Words

The words and phrases highlighted in **bold** represent key concepts in this chapter. Please take the time now to write down your definitions of these terms, using the list below and additional paper if needed. Then compare your efforts to the training text. This is an excellent way for you to determine weak points in the breadth and depth of your understanding of this chapter.

network operating system
client/server computing
NetWare
LAN Server
VINES
LAN Manager
System 7
AppleShare
global naming
X.500
directory
NetWare lite
NLM
disk mirroring
multitasking
multiprocessing
StreetTalk
Named Pipes
symmetrical multiprocessing
asymmetrical multiprocessing
peer services
NTS/2
UNIX
Windows NT

middleware
MQM
SQL
RPC
IPCs

5
MAN and WAN Internetworking

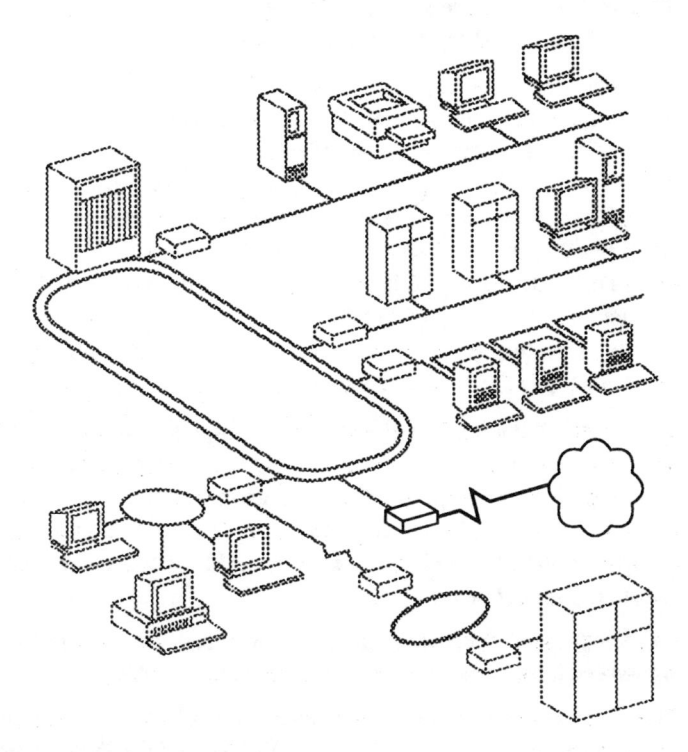

Goals of This Chapter

When you have completed this chapter, you should be able to:
- ☐ List the applications that are best suited to DQDB, SMDS, Frame Relay, ATM and SONET.
- ☐ Decide which new technologies will best serve your business needs.
- ☐ Define key technical terms used with these emerging technologies
- ☐ Define relationships between these technologies, showing how they can interoperate.

Introducing MANs

Metropolitan area networks (**MANs**) connect networks, cover areas between 6 -100 kilometers and can deliver as least 30 Mbps reliably. MAN technologies are not just bigger versions of LAN technologies because it is impossible to scale CSMA/CD or token passing technologies to the required MAN transmission speeds.

MANs are being developed to provide a higher speed, more reliable infrastructure for companies that must link LANs. Another business justification for the development of MANs is lower costs, specifically lower costs for leased lines. Network managers need the same reliability and low latency in their WANs that they have come to expect from LANs but WANs have always been network bottlenecks. Until recently, the best that a 10Mbps Ethernet manager could expect for wide area connections was a T-1 pipe at 1.544 Mbps, with all the disadvantages of a "big pipe-little pipe" intersection. With the introduction of higher speed WANs and MANs, this bottleneck will start to disappear.

To accomplish this goal, MANs must have simplified interfaces, a high degree of redundancy and provide a highly interoperable infrastructure for voice, video and data. MANs today are primarily public networks offered by local telephone companies or public carriers. As these technologies mature, some of them - notably ATM - will become popular private network choices.

On the opposite page, take some time now to consider which of these high-speed applications you need to carry in your MAN.

This chapter covers the most important emerging MAN/WAN technologies: Synchronous Optical Network (**SONET**), Distributed Queue Dual Bus (**DQDB**), Switched Multimegabit Data Service (**SMDS**), Frame Relay, Broadband Integrated Services Digital Networks (**B-ISDN**) and Asynchronous Transfer Mode (**ATM**).

All of these technologies were developed or have been approved by standards committees. For this reason, all these technologies are designed to interoporate. SONET and SMDS were developed by Bellcore and approved by ANSI in the US. Both have international equivalence. BISDN/ATM and frame relay are ISDN-family CCITT standards. DQDB came from the IEEE.

Do You Need These MAN Applications?

Advertising

CAD/CAM

Document & Image Database Access

Electronic Mail

Entertainment

High-resolution Video Database Access

Integrated Voice and Data

LAN Interconnection

Medical Imaging

Multimedia

News Retrieval

Remote Education

Security

Traffic Monitoring

Videoconferencing

Video Messaging

MAN and WAN Technologies

All the technologies discussed in this chapter fall into one of five categories: local LAN backbones, MANs, feeders from customer premises (CP) to telco facilities (central offices, COs), private WAN networks and public WAN facilities. For MANs, telcos are rolling out DQDB and SMDS. DQDB is an excellent choice for a feeder to telco. For public WANs, carriers are also offering SMDS and frame relay, ATM makes excellent sense as a high-speed WAN, but LAN vendors are also interested in ATM as a backbone for networks that need to integrate voice, video and data. None of these technologies will constitute a current competitive threat to Ethernet, Token Ring or FDDI before 1998.

The SONET specification and its international equivalent Synchronous Digital Hierarchy (**SDH**) supports both circuit and packet switched traffic. The High-speed Serial Interface (**HSSI**) supports T-1 to OC-3 (SONET) speeds for channel extension and point-to-point connections. You can economically support multiple high-bandwidth applications because they're sharing one 45 Mbps pipe. SONET is an underlying Physical Layer switching fabric for MACs like DQDB and ATM.

DQDB, the IEEE 802.6 standard, can link LANs with bandwidths from 34 Mbps to over 500Mbps. DQDB can support both circuit and packet-switched services, so it can carry voice, video and data. DQDB supports both connection-oriented and connectionless service. DQDB networks can connect to your LAN using bridges, routers and gateways. The IEEE is working on a multiport bridge standard for DQDB.

SMDS specifies a connectionless packet service over a cell-switching MAC. You can mix SMDS with most standards-based Physical Layer technologies. The first roll-outs by telcos and interexchange carriers will implement SMDS over T-3 or DQDB. By 1996 it should be available over SONET, FDDI and B-ISDN.

Standard ISDN cannot serve the gigabit data transport needs of MAN customers, but B-ISDN can. The B-ISDN model includes ATM as it's Physical and Data Link Layers. You are expected to put SONET under ATM.

Technologies and Services: What Works Together Today?

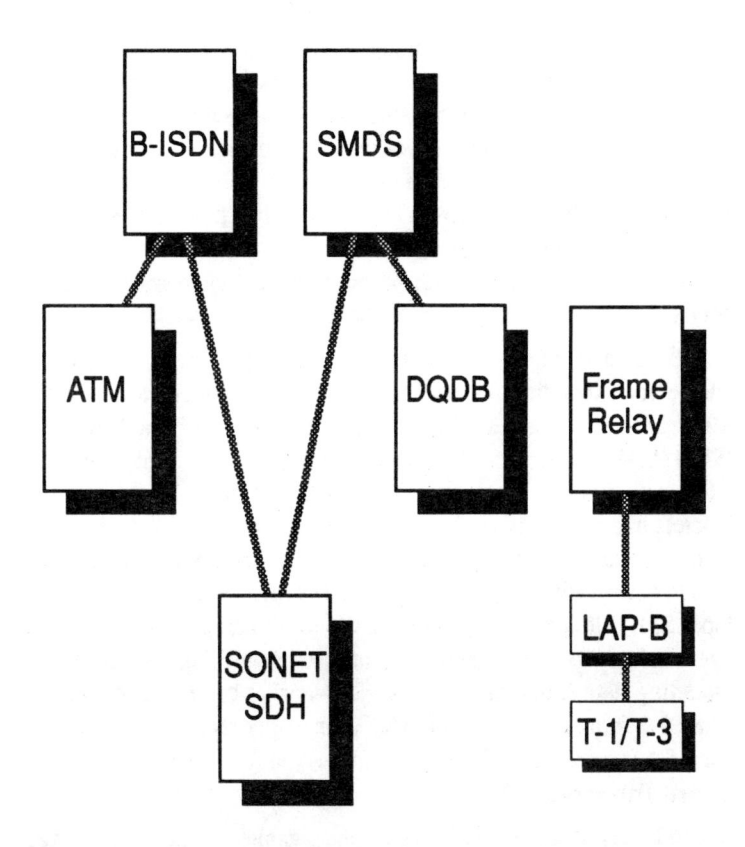

[Diagram showing B-ISDN and SMDS connecting down to ATM, DQDB; ATM and DQDB connecting to SONET/SDH; Frame Relay connecting to LAP-B and T-1/T-3]

This illustration shows how the various Physical and MAC technologies can be used with upper layer services today. All the Physical/MAC technologies were designed by standards groups so they are designed to interoperate. Boxes show relationships and are not to scale.

Your SONET Switching Fabric

The ANSI SONET standard defines 4 layers of function within OSI's Physical Layer. The Photonic Layer transports bits and converts electrical STS signals to optical carrier (OC) signals. It requires 1310 or 1550 nanometer laser optical transceivers. The Section Layer transports frames to the first repeater and then from repeater to repeater. The Line Layer transports frames from one major switching element to the next and the Path Layer provides a reliable interface to other protocols above the SONET layers. A path takes a frame from one user premises to another. Each of these layers has it's own overhead in the SONET frame, which is a lot of overhead but it allows different organizations (carriers, customers) to manage portions of the transmission independently. SONET was introduced in *Mastering Internetworking*.

SONET's basic unit of transport is signal transport service 1 (STS-1) whose corresponding optical carrier 1 (OC-1) service carries 51.84 Mbps in North America. The CCITT Synchronous Digital Hierarchy (SDH) basic rate of 155.52 Mps equals SONET's OC-3 rate. An STS-1 frame diagram usually show octets in 9 rows by 90 columns. The first 3 octets in each row are overhead, 3 rows of section and 6 of line. The path overhead is 9 octets, carried with the payload. Normally, this begins in octet position 4 but if the payload (Synchronous Payload Envelope, SPE) "floats" it may start elsewhere. Floating mode, with path overhead and its SPE, is a critical feature of SONET in a WAN, where incoming data flows can arrive slightly earlier or later than expected.STS-1 frames are transmitted 8000 times per second just like standard T-1 frames. An STS-1 frame can carry slower traffic (like T-1) in Virtual Tributaries (VTs).

SONET can reach potential speeds in the gigabits/second (Gbps) at OC levels up to 96. SONET multiplexes to these speeds by concatenating overhead and interleaving bytes. Future telco services will ride on SONET because of these speeds, because of the separation of overhead into separately managable portions and because SONET carries bits without regard to the type of service represented by the bits. This means that you can run voice, data, video or imaging transparently as long as the traffic is digital. In particular, SONET can accommodate many different MACs including FDDI, ATM, 802.6 and DQDB.

Section, Line and Path

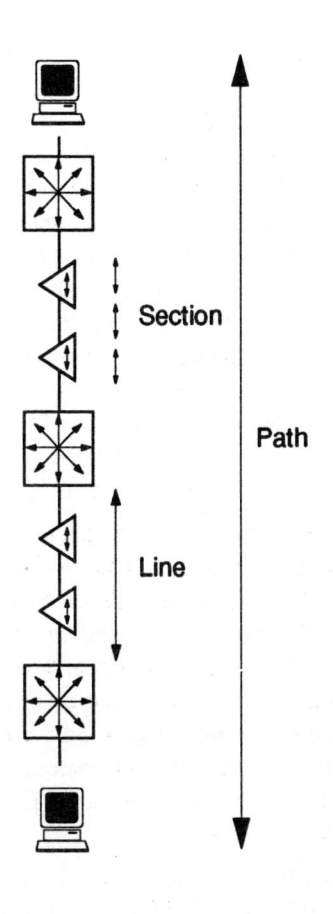

Packet, Circuit and Cell switching

Before we move on to examine technologies in detail, let's spend some time looking at the business reasons behind the development of **cell switching**.Neither circuit switching nor packet switching can serve all of a network manager's needs so most companies have used both types of switching in separate backbones. You use circuit-switched technology for voice calls and other applications that require guaranteed bandwidth or low latency. Bursty data is more suited to packet switching because it uses bandwidth efficiently and because latency doesn't matter (within reason). It's difficult to send voice and video over packet-switched WAN links and end up happy with the results because of the variable delay intrinsic to packet switching. If the data traffic is heavy enough, you can put packet traffic onto a circuit switching network. For instance, a T-1 mux with a circuit switching infrastructure can use its circuits for data packets if the circuits connect routers for LAN to LAN traffic. Communications heaven, of course, involves a solution that allows you to integrate all of your traffic using one switching scheme or at least one backbone.

Since we need to create network infrastructures that can reliably and manageably carry isochronous as well a data traffic, **cell switching** offers the best hope for this integration. Let's use ATM as an example of cell switching here. ATM cell switching grew out of early work on fast packet switching. As our digital transmission facilities have become more reliable, network switches don't need to check for errors on every hop. ATM puts its information into small, fixed sized cells that are very easy to switch quickly. You can assign a guaranteed number of cells per time interval for isochronous traffic and let bursty LAN applications fill up the remaining cells.

ATM specifies classes of service to accommodate both isochronous and time-insensitive traffic and defines virtual channels for end-to-end error control. ATM headers include a Cell Loss Priority (**CLP**) field so that the network can preferentially dump low priority traffic in case of congestion.Each ATM cell is 53 octets long with a 5 octet header and 48 octets of payload. SMDS uses the exact same payload size. (Isn't standards coordination wonderful?) We'll discuss both these technologies in detail later.

MANs and WANs

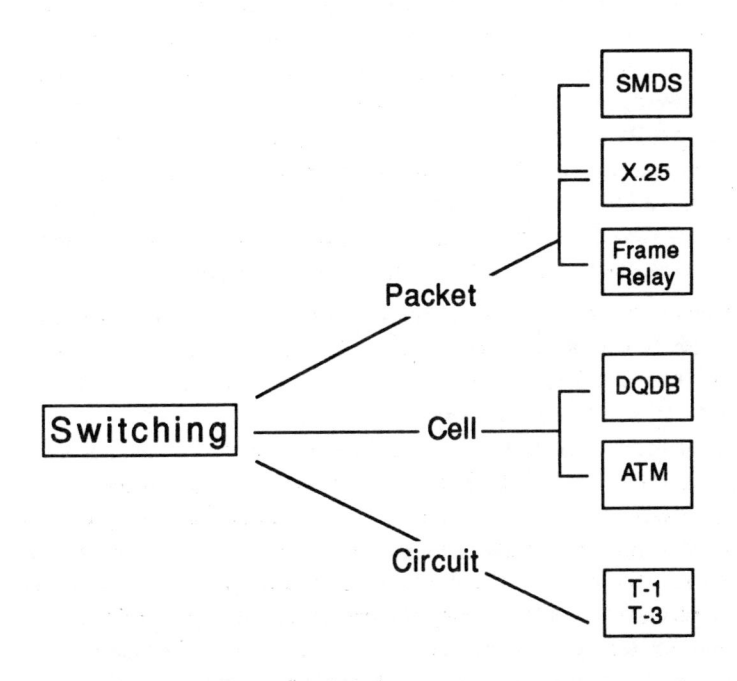

```
                          ┌── SMDS
                   Packet─┼── X.25
                          └── Frame Relay
Switching ────── Cell ────┬── DQDB
                          └── ATM
                 Circuit───── T-1
                              T-3
```

DQDB Technology

DQDB uses two buses coexisting on the same wire and moving data in opposite directions. If node 12 needs to send data to node 29, it must put the data on bus A while the reply from 29 to 12 will be carried on bus B. In this case, bus A is called the forward bus, and bus B is called the **reverse bus**. Each bus has an active component called the head of bus (**HOB**). The head of one bus is the end of the other bus. DQDB carries data (payloads) in slots, which are created by the HOB. Each slot carries a 1 octet Access Control Field (**ACF**) and a 52 octet payload segment. The DQDB bandwidth is completely divided into slots, without the periods of silence that a CSMA/CD LAN contains.

Regular data moves in **QA** (Queued Arbitrated) **slots**. A node with data to send on bus A sets a **request bit** in the first slot passing on bus B. In order to send data, the node has to queue up for a slot and has to wait until all its downstream neighbors—those who are ahead of it in the queue—have had a chance to send before it can send. Each node has a **Request Counter** that counts the number of request bits it sees on the reverse bus so if you want to send on A, you will count the request bits on B. If you have data to send, you set a request bit on the reverse bus, set your **Countdown Counter** to equal whatever your Request Counter value currently is (how many stations are ahead of you in the queue) and then set the Request Counter back to zero. Every time the Request Counter sees an empty slot on the forward bus it knows that the empty slot will service one of its downstream neighbors and it decreases its Countdown Counter by one. When the Countdown Counter reaches zero, the next empty slot belongs to you!

The HOB sets aside **PA** (Pre-Arbitrated) slots for isochronous traffic. PA slots are not allocated to a single node like QA slots are. Nodes using PA slots read virtual circuit (VC) numbers in the slot header to determine if the data in the slot corresponds to a VC they are currently using. Various nodes use specific **octet positions** within the slot for reading and writing data. In this way, time-sensitive traffic is guaranteed enough bandwidth.

You can run a DQDB bus between a single router and a CO. In this case, you have no contention for slots. Some users may use this local DQDB as a feeder to connect to a CO running a public DQDB. What DQDB calls a slot is a cell in ATM.

DQDB Uses a Dual Bus

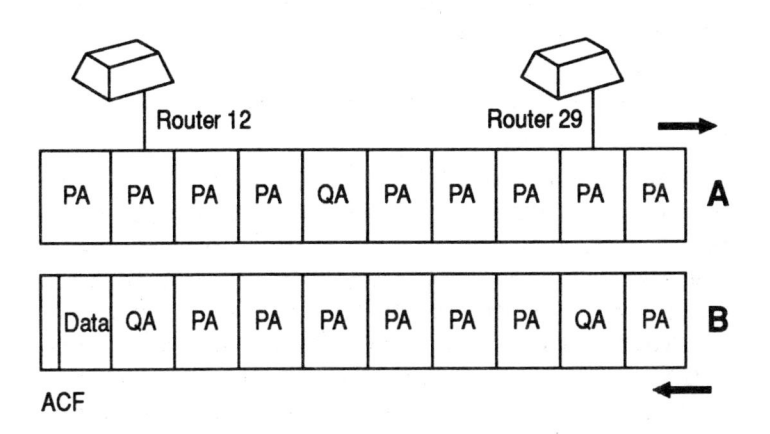

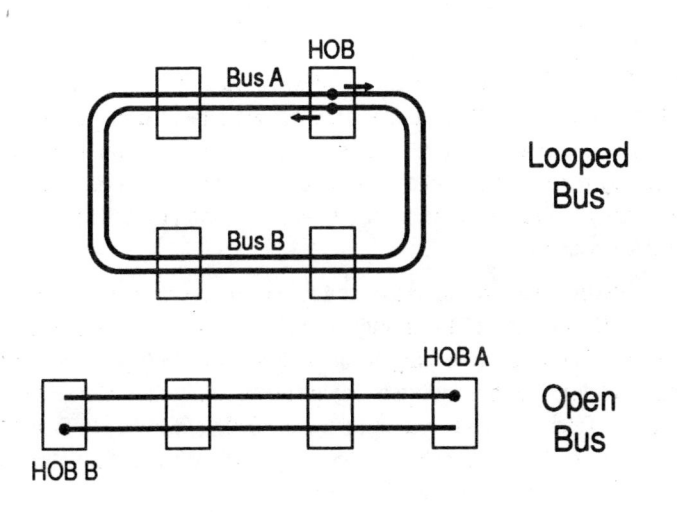

Looped Bus

Open Bus

SMDS Service Interfaces

SMDS is an exciting new service now being rolled out by the public carriers. The point where the customer premises intersects with the SMDS network is called the Subscriber Network Interface (**SNI**). SMDS expects a single point of entry from the customer network to the public network. SNI exists within a router, CSU/DSU or similar device.

The SMDS Interface Protocol (SIP) defines 3 levels of function for private network access to SMDS. It has no flow control or error recovery but it can detect errors. SIP Level 3 interfaces with various LLCs, including 802.2 for Ethernet, Token Ring and FDDI. The SMDS packet assembly process begins when a LAN packet arrives at a router. The router puts the packet into SMDS envelope, then fragments into cells. (SMDS assumes it will have DQDB or another cell relay Physical/MAC transport under it and some of the SMDS specs include these lower layers.) Header, trailer plus 9188 octets of user packet comprises the SMDS data unit.

Since SMDS implements connectionless service, the network utilizes its bandwidth very efficiently. SMDS carries a large user payload so LAN packets can be carried without fragmentation. It's important for efficiency reasons that packets not fragment in the SMDS network because fragmentation and reassembly increases the processing load on the LAN routers.

The network–network interface, called the Interexchange Carrier Interface (**ICI**), connects local telco switches to interexchange carrier switches. The Inter-Switching Systems Interface (**ISSI**) connects different vendor switches within a single carrier network, for example if Northern Telecom and Ericsson both sell SMDS switches to Bell Atlantic. If routers at both ends of the connection conform to SNI, the two end users will be able to communicate.

What will happen in many networks is that a router (DTE) will pass the data flow to a DSU/CSU (DCE) which will make the actual physical connection via SNI to the SMDS switch. The connection between the router and the DSU/CSU is the Data Exchange Interface (**DXI**). You can expect vendors to incorporate as many interfaces as possible in a single box, as the network integration process continues. Router vendors are working on direct physical interfaces to SMDS switches and putting DXI and SNI in their boxes.

The SMDS Data Structure

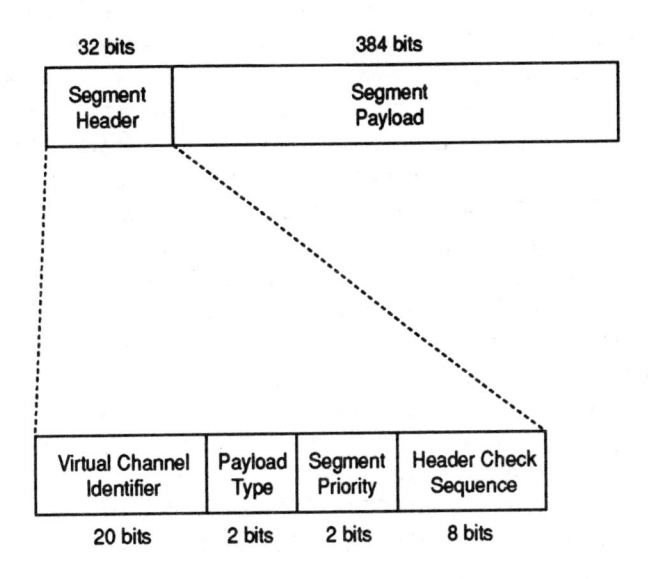

32 bits	384 bits
Segment Header	Segment Payload

Virtual Channel Identifier	Payload Type	Segment Priority	Header Check Sequence
20 bits	2 bits	2 bits	8 bits

Subscriber Network Interface

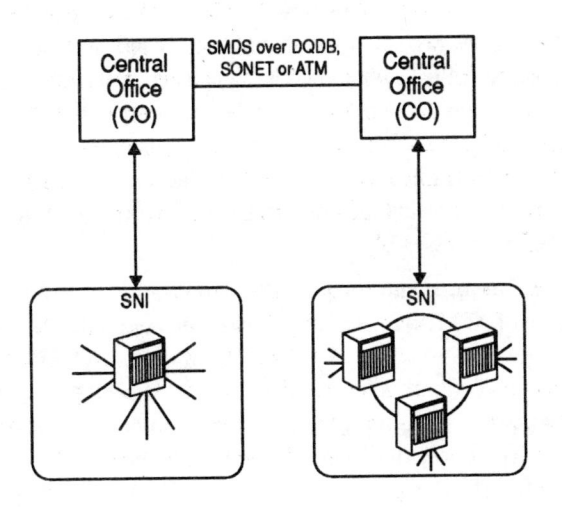

The Broadband ISDN Model

The B-ISDN model supports class A and B service for voice and video and classes C and D for data. The Physical Layer of the model is assumed to be SONET, although early implementations have been rolled out over T-3. This Physical Layer, with its two sublayers, interfaces to the ATM Layer, which acts as a MAC. The **ATM Layer** is service independent and defines the cell structure and how a cell flows over the network. The ATM Layer creates Virtual Channel Connections (**VCCs**) which can be grouped into a Virtual Path Connection (**VPC**). Each VCC will have traffic descriptors associated with it to define expected cell rates. The ATM **Adaptation Layer** (AAL) is service dependent and makes it possible to multiplex various types of circuit and packet switching traffic onto the same data path. Each class has a separate AAL, with AAL 5 in development for high-speed data. The AALs convert packet or circuit-switched traffic into cells and handle cell loss errors. Within the Adaptation Layer, the Segmentation and Reassembly (SAR) sublayer takes the ATM Layer's cells and reassembles frames and circuits (in a basic way) while the Convergence Sublayer (which has its own two sublayers!) provides interfacing to the specific classes of service. The Adaptation Layer interfaces directly to higher layer services like IP or SMDS.

Your premises network interacts with a CO ATM switch at the Adaptation Layer whose two sublayers assemble cells and pass them on to the ATM Layer for actual switching. The switch puts cells into its outgoing stream depending on their VCCs. At the receiving end, the switch accepts cells and passes them on to the PBX or router associated with the VCC after it has turned them back into packets or voice calls. If cells are damaged, the switch communicates error recovery to the sending switch before re-assembly.

The ATM Forum, an informal industry group working to speed up development of ATM products, has published two interface standards: the User to Network Interface (**UNI**) and Network to Network Interface (**NNI**). If two vendors conform to these standards, their products should interoperate for signalling, physical media interface and basic cell functions. The Forum recommends the Q.93B standard for signalling, a relative of ISDN's Q.931.

ATM Standard

	Class A Constant Bit Rate Circuit Emulation	Class B Variable Bit Rate Audio/Video	Class C Connection Oriented Services for Data	Class D Connection- less Services for Data
	AAL 1	AAL 2	AAL 3	AAL 4
			AAL 5	

ATM Standard

- **Adaptation Layer**
  - Convergence Sub-Layer
  - Segmentation & Reassembly Sub-Layer
- **ATM Layer**
- **Physical Layer**
  - Transmission Convergence Sub-Layer
  - Physical Medium Sub-Layer

Planning An ATM Strategy

ATM scales easily, which means that you can add additional switching elements and create a more richly-meshed node without impacting performance. The fact that switches are handling fixed sized cells makes it easy to scale data rates. As your network size increases, your network management burden should increase proportionately rather than geometrically.

Remember that ATM is most appropriate for trunk and backbone networks operating at 100 Mbps or more. And don't plan to use ATM service at low speeds. Because the ATM switch must wait to send a cell until the cell is full, 64 kb pipes will time out applications before they can fill a cell. At 64 kb, there is a 6 ms. delay at each end of the circuit.- The new technology called "Isochronous Ethernet", based on the IEEE 802.9 standard, uses standard ISDN B channels for isochronous traffic running parallel to the Ethernet bus. It may give you better results than ATM for your voice/video at low speeds.

If you're considering using ATM as part of your networking strategy, you've probably considered ATM either as a LAN backbone (hub of hubs) or as a WAN. Only the most visionary analysts are recommending that you trash your existing premises infrastructure and replace it with ATM switches. Those that do may be overselling for your needs at this time. Ethernet switching, FDDI and other high-speed alternatives exist with proven track records. ATM is most appropriate as a backbone.

ATM switch vendors are starting to roll out products in all these areas. **Access speeds** (from your router to the switch) are generally no faster than T-1, while trunking speeds vary from T-3 to OC-3. Most router vendors are introducing ATM products. One vendor is implementing an interface to the DSU, while others are putting OC-3 cards into the router or moving to an ATM backplane. Most vendors are taking a phased approach to ATM and this makes sense. Few network managers have the opportunity to junk their entire existing equipment base every time a new technology comes along.

ATM Switching

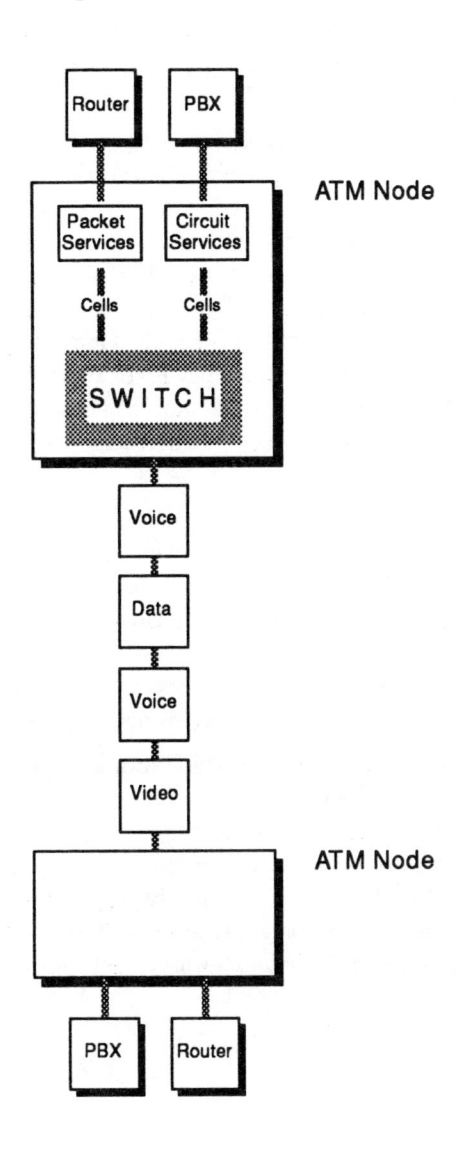

Frame Relay – Part 2

In *Mastering Internetworking*, we explored most of the basic technology of frame relay. Let's move on to explore performance issues, management and interoperability.

Most frame relay vendors find that their frame relay access devices (**FRADs**) need to support sophisticated forms of **bursting**. In burst mode, your router (or other access device) allows a user to greatly exceed their CIR for a time. How extended the bursts are allowed to be, that is, how long and how many Mb over the CIR, determines how sophisticated your burst capacity is. Some vendors will allow you to take up the entire pipe, if wide area links are idle momentarily as they are likely to be between midnight and dawn, for example. Your vendor might also allow you to sign up for wide-area bandwidth exceeding your CIR, allowing you to burst but only charge you for your actual usage.

RFC 1294 defines specifications for how routers interact with the frame relay network; essentially the VC structure creates tunnels from router to router. Things get interesting in multiprotocol routing. Do you create separate VCs for each protocol and potentially waste bandwidth? Or do you multiplex the various protocols onto the same VC? Obviously if you multiplex at one end you need to demultiplex at the other. A lot depends on the frame relay carrier's pricing structure.

Many frame relay customers use SNMP as a universal management protocol. These customers are interested in integrating their premises management with frame relay performance management. Some vendors are using OSPF as the mechanism for rerouting virtual circuits in the event of path failure. (Most vendors use proprietary algorithms.) If the network and your customer premises both use OSPF, they may eventually be able to communicate management information.

Burst Mode

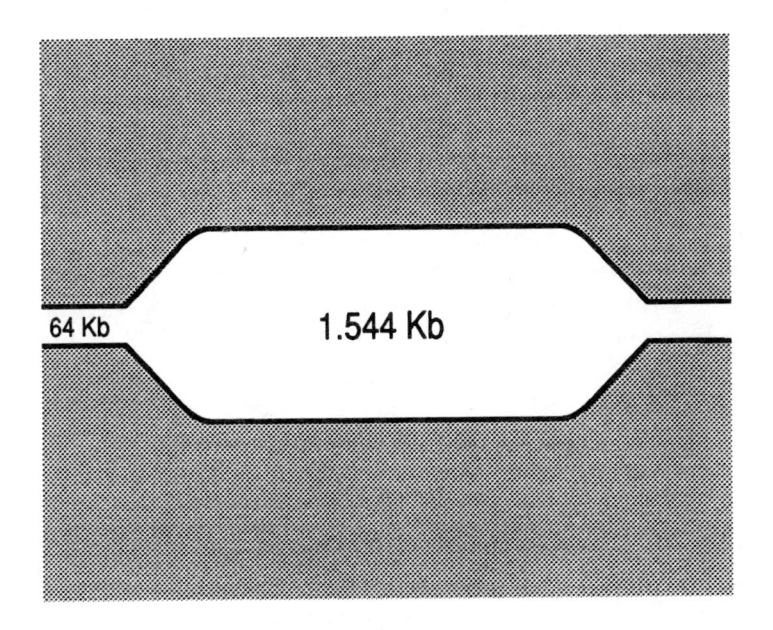

A subscriber momentarily bursts from DS-0 (its CIR) to an entire DS-1.

Public or Private Network

As with other existing technologies, you can make choices on whether you want your high-speed MAN/WAN to be a private network that you build and maintain yourself or public network capacity that you lease. The Physical Layer technologies can be purchased for private network creation (SONET, ATM) while the Data Link and higher level services, as well as DQDB, are a public network phenomenon. Very few network managers are finding purely private networks cost-effective at this time. Most managers are experimenting with public network offerings from the local Bell companies and the interexchange carriers. The biggest boost to the public network offerings will be usage-based pricing. The possibility of ending up leasing more capacity than they need or not being able to nimbly respond to sudden changes in traffic levels (the bursting issue, for example) makes some managers reluctant to invest. Most of the public networks offer virtual network options where, just as with earlier services, you can create a pseudo-private network using public facilities.

You can use the checklist in *Mastering Internetworking* to help you decide which network type to investigate. When dealing with technologies that are as new as the technologies described in this chapter, I recommend caution when proceding with private network purchases. Unless you have a very technically-savvy and experienced staff, public or virtual private options will give you more than enough challenge.

Instead of making an either/or choice, you can create a WAN composed of public and private components, for instance, a routed campus internet connected to public frame relay, a virtual private SMDS—both for long distance transport—and a public MAN. Regardless of whether your network is public or private, if you are integrating technologies you must consider management and security issues, especially your ability to integrate private and public management information, as well as migration strategies for integrating technologies both today and tomorrow.

Which Applications?

As you can see, the emerging technologies can carry your existing LAN–LAN applications and most future applications as well.

Applications	SONET	DQDB	ATM	Frame Relay	SMDS
video, hi-bandwidth	✔	✔	✔	■	■
video, lo-bandwidth	✔	✔	✔	■	■
term/host	✔	✔	✔	✔	✔
PC/Workstation to WS	✔	✔	✔	✔	✔
teleconferencing	✔	✔	✔	■	■
desktop teleconferencing	✔	✔	✔	■	■
file transfer (large)	✔	✔	✔	✔	✔
short, interactive	✔	✔	✔	✔	✔
server/server	✔	✔	✔	✔	✔
Mainframe/MF	✔	✔	✔	✔	✔
voice	✔	✔	✔	■	■

Physical Layer, then MAC, then packet level technologies are listed left to right for easy comparison.

Most technologies **can** carry voice or video if it is digitized. You may not experience minimal acceptable performance levels.

■ no

✔ yes

Integrating MAN/WAN Technologies

To make the best decisions for your corporate network, you need to ignore a great deal of the either/or mentality common to vendors and (occasionally) analysts. Trying a little bit of everything will certainly drive you crazy but you can mix technologies and services to get a well-designed structure for your corporate information without worrying overmuch about interoperability if you know what your real needs are and keep your decision-making balanced between caution and enthusiasm. Like the four humors of the ancient Greeks, letting either tendency get out of control will lead you to disaster.

The various MAN technologies can interoperate with each other but they have, in many cases, radically different designs and were created for different constituencies. This means that comparing them directly can be an apples to aardvarks comparison. DQDB, for instance is a Physical and Mac Layer technology specification, while SMDS defines a higher level packet service that was designed to be implemented on top of DQDB. Maximum frame sizes and formats vary: frame relay can handle Ethernet but possibly not token ring; SMDS with 9188 octets of payload can handle anything, even FDDI; ATM's AAL5 can support up to 64,000 octet frames, divided into cells. Performance degrades and errors can occur if a router can't put an entire packet into another service's payload and it has to fragment packets, so you should work hard to avoid fragmentation.

Bellcore is doing conformance testing for DQDB, SMDS and ATM but there is no formal certification process to guarantee interoperability. The various telcos are working on interoperability with the interexchange carriers.

One option we haven't discussed that you may consider for LAN backbones is good old FDDI with data compression. The **FDDI-II** standard can carry isochronous traffic just like ATM: too bad it isn't compatible with original FDDI! For non-backbone use, the FDDI protocols are migrating to twisted pair wire from various vendors. There are also three proposals for 100 Mbps Ethernet now being considered by the 802.3 committee.

Integrating ATM with IP/IPX

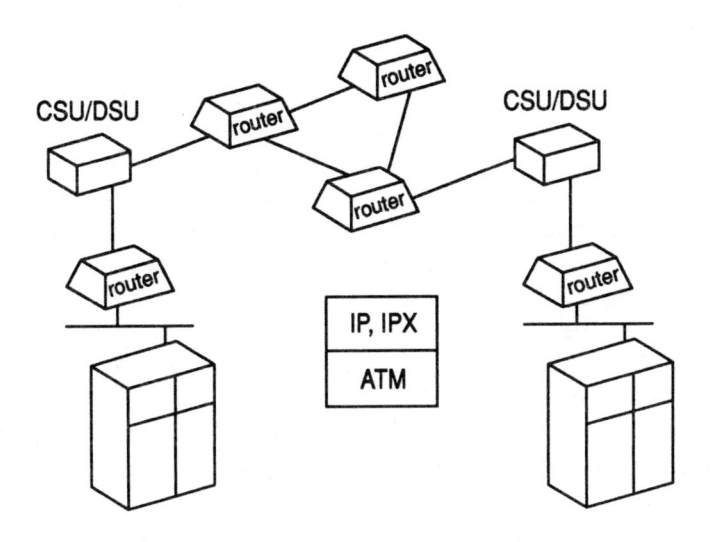

Integrating Frame Relay with IP/IPX

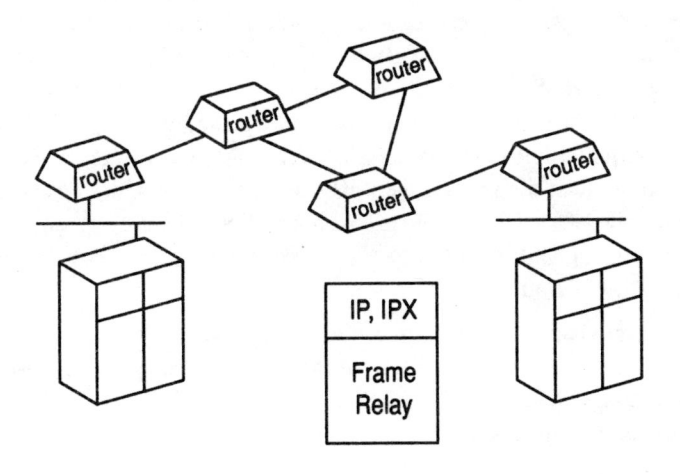

Managing an Integrated MAN/WAN

Management is the great frontier when integrating technologies and, as always, standards are welcome. Frame relay switching management, specifically information on PVC status, is covered in ANSI P1.617 Annex D. **Annex D** management is different from the Link Management Interface (LMI) approved by the Frame Relay Forum, a group of working vendors and users. **LMI** as well as Annex D address the need for active management information flow between network nodes and the routers on the customer premises that create frame relay flows. ANSI T1.606 Addendum 1 defines FECN, BECN and DE, the mechanisms that we currently have for flow control and performance management. According to LMI, the status of all active DLCIs must be reported within one 1400 byte frame, which means that you can have no more than 360 active DLCIs per port. Some network managers will discover problems with this limit in SNA networks with traditional terminal to host traffic. The IETF RFC 1294 defines how you encapsulate IP and other protocols across frame relay.

Congestion affects all network types and is one of the major ongoing issues in MAN and WAN service development. In fact, congestion and flow management are the major reasons why applications perform badly, not interoperability problems per se. Quality of service guarantees are essential if you are trying to deliver isochronous service. In DQDB isochronous services get guaranteed bandwidth with PA slots. SMDS includes control information to allow low priority traffic to be dumped if needed. ATM has the CLP field. Most of these strategies have not been well tested in working networks. Interoperability on a public network requires that all parties behave "fairly", that is, they don't exceed the traffic load the network expects. Every public provider has their own strategy for dealing with excess traffic. Some vendors' strategy is to do nothing and just let congestion happen; the police officer role is left to the CP routers.

When provisioning these new services, especially the connectionless services, carriers have to plan for maximum, not average, data flows. When using SMDS, your local networks need to use TCP, TP-4 or other error recovery protocols.

MAN/WAN Management

☐ How do you manage congestion to maximize performance?

Frame relay	FECN, BECN, DE, CIR, Burst
ATM	CLP
DQDB	PA slots
SMDS	Quality of service (QOS)

☐ Maximum data flows need to be provided for
  • Consider QOS management issues as you deploy these technologies for your business critical technologies
  • When provisioning these new services, especially the connectionless services, carriers have to plan for maximum, not average, data flows.

☐ When using SMDS, your local networks need to use TCP, TP-4 or other error recovery protocols.

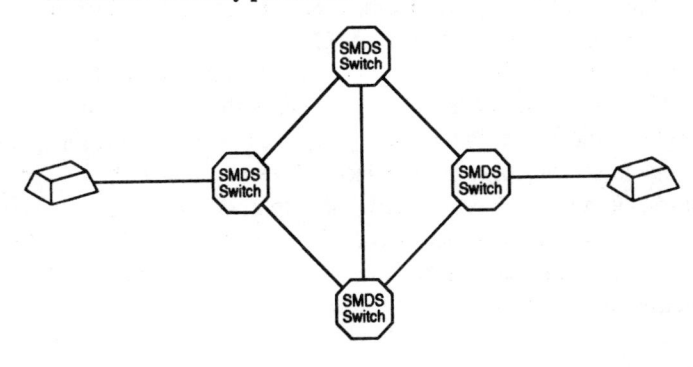

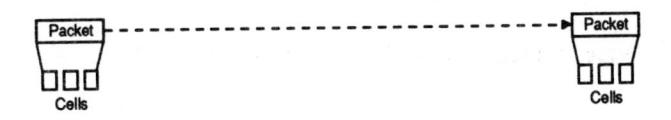

A Tale of Two Network Managers

Bob has a network with multimedia applications joining his CAD/CAM operations with a routed backbone connecting Ethernets. The increased load is choking his network. His network includes offices in Chicago, Detroit, Dallas and Washington D.C. At some point in the future (in the next century, he hopes) he will be responsible for the voice network which is currently running over T-1 circuits with 19.2 Kbps backups. He needs more capacity, better management and performance tuning for his routed internet, and he needs to consider future needs.

- Give him some advice. What specific features does his solution require?

- What technologies should he investigate? WHY?

Sadie has been blessed with the management of a 6-city internetwork in southern California; five facilities have standardized on Ethernet and one holdout (who plays golf with the CFO) insists on Token Rings. The Ethernet cities use NetWare and VINES with existing servers. Sadie's mandate is a migration to client/server applications, which has passed its pilot project with flying colors. She is now implementing an application downsizing plan that will move all remaining mainframe applications to a server-based architecture. To complete her downsizing successfully in management's eyes, the users need to experience low latency, which means that both her local networks and her WAN connections need more bandwidth.

- Give her some advice. What specific features does her solution require?

- What technologies should she investigate? WHY?

ARCHITECTURES REVIEW

Bob's Network

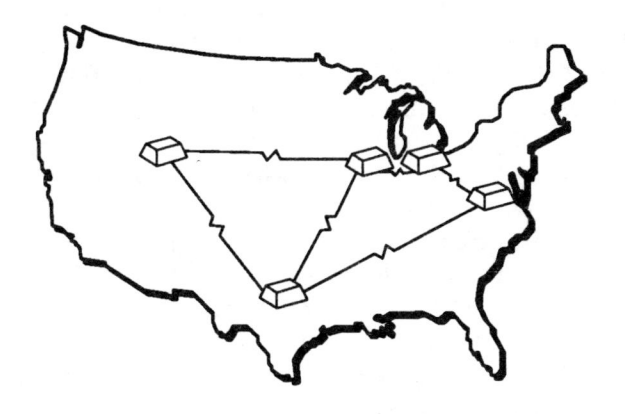

Sadie's Network

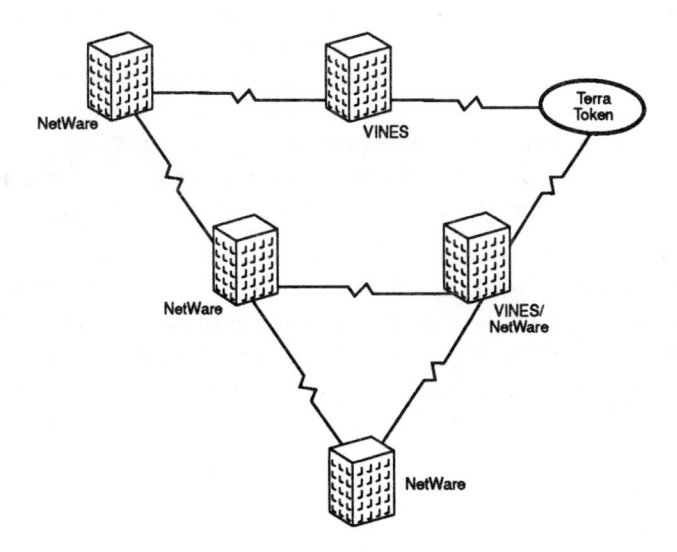

Looking to the Future

Technology integration is certainly making integrated networking easier. For instance, T-1 multiplexors are being introduced with frame relay and SMDS interfaces, integrated bridge/routers have ATM, SONET and SMDS interfaces and the same routers that tout their backplanes as a collapsed backbone include interfaces to ATM, SMDS and other backbone technologies. Some switch manufacturers are offering hybrid switches that can switch more than one technology. These vendors generally implement native switching using one preferred technology—a SONET switch that can also move ATM traffic, for instance. There will probably be performance differences between a switch that performs native ATM switching and one that includes ATM interfaces but performs native proprietary or frame relay switching. Since there will certainly be pricing differences between the two approaches, you have to be careful not to let initial cost issues blind you to architecture (long-term cost) issues.

The migration of technology to boards and integratable chips will give you more options. Several intelligent hub manufacturers have board level versions of all these technologies for integration with local structured wiring. The hub backplanes therefore are concentrating both local and wide area traffic. A hub that contains not only local connections but also frame relay, ATM, SMDS and other WAN switching will collapse your backbone, may make management easier but will give you a single point of failure unless you take advantage of maximum redundancy. Vendor consortia are working on SONET and ATM chip sets.

Both technology and services are exploding in this area, offering you additional choices every month. Hopefully, this chapter will have given you the basic information and the structure that you need to make your decisions wisely, without being overly swayed by the glamour or the rhetoric of a particular vendor or technology forum.

Your MAN/WAN Strategy

Image networking, LAN internetworking and higher speeds. That's why network managers are interested in MANs, in published surveys by the Yankee Group.

☐ Why are **you** considering a new MAN/WAN strategy?
    _____
    _____
    _____

☐ What are your most critical **business needs** at this time?
  - Lower WAN costs
  - Lower management costs (integrated management of existing technologies would help)

    _____
    _____
    _____

☐ Which of these **business needs** do you think a new strategy will serve?
    _____
    _____
    _____

☐ What Physical Layer **technologies** are you considering?
    _____
    _____
    _____

☐ What **services** are you considering?

☐ How will you phase these new technologies into your network plan? (In stages? All at once?)

☐ Do a before and after diagram of your WAN, showing the integration of your new technology. Fine tune your strategy, providing backups and redundancy.

Summary

- The major business justification for MANs is lower cost and increased reliability for LAN-LAN traffic.
- MANs deliver voice, data and video reliably at speeds over 34 Mbps and interoperability with LANs over standard interfaces.
- DQDB is a MAC technology using a dual queued bus that was designed to carry SMDS over it (for data only).
- DQDB is the IEEE 802.6 standard and offers bandwidth from 34–500 Mbps. DQDB can support both isochronous and standard traffic. SMDS supports connectionless packet transmission using 53-octet cells.
- SONET and SDH support both circuit and packet switching. SONET is a Physical Layer ANSI standard.
- Broadband ISDN includes ATM, a popular emerging cell relay technology with 53-octet cells. B-ISDN was developed to interoperate with 802.6 and SONET.
- The MAN market is growing rapidly, approaching $1.3 billion.

Review – Chapter 5

1. What two technologies in this chapter do you think you will implement most quickly? How (specifically) will they help your business?
2. Name 3 MAN or WAN services that have been rolled out almost exclusively by telco and common carriers.
3. What characteristics of DQDB/SMDS make it a good choice for public networks?
4. ATM was designed to operate over what Physical Layer technology?
5. SMDS was designed to operate over which technology?

ARCHITECTURES REVIEW

6. Name the standards organization(s) responsible for SONET, ATM and frame relay.
7. What is the IEEE MAN standard? List the number and name.
8. In a DQDB MAN, if a station wishes to send data to another station on bus A, it must put its request on bus ____
9. DQDB puts isochronous services into (PA/QA) slots.
10. Describe the method by which DQDB guarantees fair access to the bandwidth for all stations. (In other words, describe how DQDB works.)
11. Which technologies allow you to integrate voice and data?
12. How does ATM manage congestion?
13. The ATM cell is ____ in length of which ____ is header.
14. Which technologies discussed here are connection-oriented? Why do you care?
15. What does SONET stand for?
16. Can SONET carry isochronous traffic? Why or why not?
17. Name the three components of SONET overhead and state specifically what portion of the network they manage.
18. SONET service in Europe is called ____ with a payload starting at ____ Mbps.
19. Can frame relay be implemented over SONET? Why or why not?
20. Is ATM an effective "frame relay killer"? Why or why not? Be specific.
21. Which technology discussed here is easily interfaced with FDDI? What makes the interface easy?
22. ____ is a connectionless packet service for wide area use.
23. How does existing T-1 networking fit into the emerging technologies discussed in this chapter?
24. Why is ATM most appropriate for backbones today?
25. What ATM layer actually switches cells through the network?

Key Words

The words and phrases highlighted in **bold** represent key concepts in this chapter. Please take the time now to write down your own definitions of these terms, using the list below and additional paper if needed. Then compare your efforts to the training text. This is an excellent way for you to determine weak points in the breadth and depth of your understanding of this chapter.

MANs	DXI
SONET	cell switching
DQDB	cells
SMDS	CLP
B-ISDN	ATM Layer
ATM	VCCs
SDH	VPC
payload	Adaptation Layer
HSSI	UNI
reverse bus	NNI
HOB	access speeds
ACF	FRADs
QA slots	bursting
Request counter	FDDI-II
request bit	Annex D
Countdown Counter	LMI
PA	
octet positions	
SNI	
ICI	
ISSI	

6
Backbones & Multi-Protocol Internets

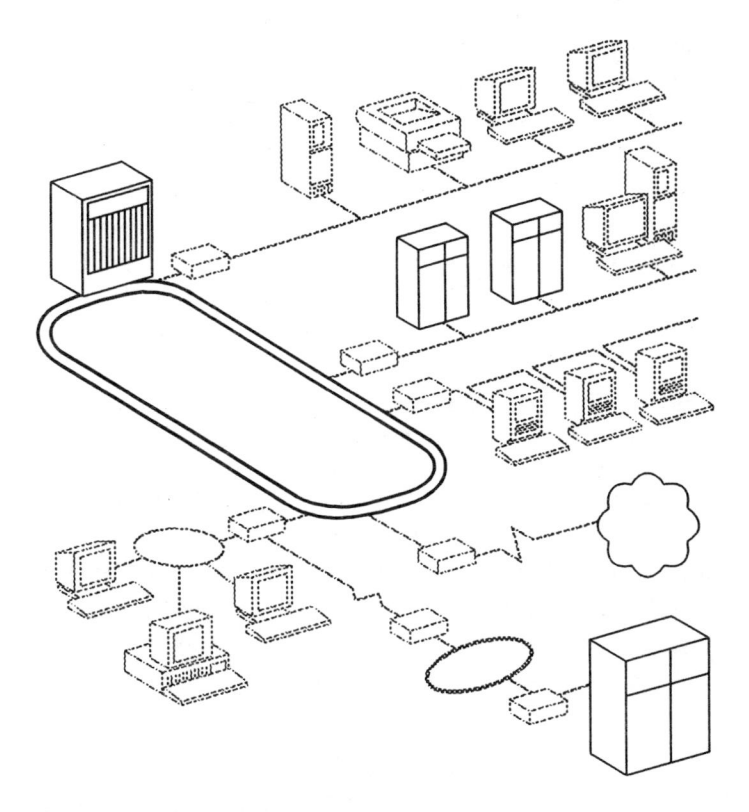

Goals of this Chapter

When you have completed this chapter you will be able to:
- ❐ List 3 major architectures involved in multi-protocol networks
- ❐ List 2 strategies for internetworking multiple architectures
- ❐ List 3 major components of the new SNA and strategies for SNA interoperability
- ❐ Define a collapsed backbone and determine whether this architecture is best for your network

Why Multi-Protocol?

The architectures most often involved in multi-protocol internetworking are all discussed in this chapter: TCP/IP, SNA, DECnet, AppleTalk, OSI and Novell. Depending on the applications involved, you may need to internetwork at the Data Link Layer (bridging, tunnelling or conversion), at the Network Layer (using routers), through a NOS or middleware, or through an application gateway. A distributed computing software architecture allows you to create and access applications regardless of the underlying transport.

When developing your multi-protocol strategy, keep in mind that delivering the best possible service to the end users is your real mandate—it won't matter how much money you saved if response time and reliability don't support the major corporate goal of making money. (Marney-Petix' first law of business: saving money is nice but making money is critical.)

This chapter will survey the various ways you can develop linkages between network architectures and help you to decide which strategies are appropriate for your business. You will also have an opportunity to look at performance issues in multi-protocol networks and consider migration strategies from one architecture to another. Since backbone architecture has a huge impact on performance, you will also have an opportunity to develop a personalized backbone strategy.

Multi-Protocol Networking

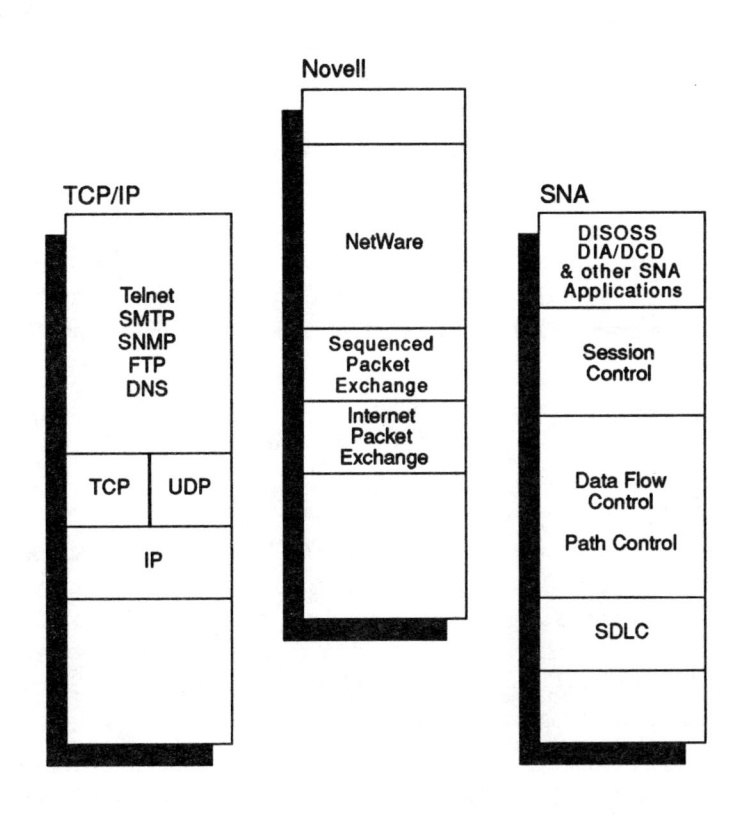

TCP/IP
- Telnet
- SMTP
- SNMP
- FTP
- DNS

| TCP | UDP |

IP

Novell
- NetWare
- Sequenced Packet Exchange
- Internet Packet Exchange

SNA
- DISOSS DIA/DCD & other SNA Applications
- Session Control
- Data Flow Control
- Path Control
- SDLC

Introducing Backbones

If you have more than 100 devices and you're carrying mission-critical applications, you need a backbone. Backbones should only carry LAN–LAN traffic and protect individual LANs from problems elsewhere in the network. You need a backbone to segment traffic so that local traffic does not proliferate beyond the local network. A good backbone design follows these rules:

• Nothing but concentrators or internet devices should connect to a backbone.

• Put mainframes and servers on a dedicated LAN segment rather than directly on a backbone. Putting them directly on the backbone makes the most critical element of your network reliability strategy more failure prone.

(Other analysts are less stringent and will put servers, mainframes and other "global service providers" on the backbone.)

Your backbone has a technology and a topology. LAN to LAN backbones are frequently Ethernet, 16 Mbps Token Ring and FDDI while WAN backbones rely on SMDS and SONET. Your local backbones can be **risers** (running vertically, floor to floor, within a building), or run horizontally on a single floor. They can even be collapsed within a device—router, switch or intelligent hub. Your wider-area backbones can be a campus ring, a mesh of routers covering the continental U.S. or a high-speed international connection.

Backbone topologies can be buses (horizontal or vertical), rings, meshes and stars. WAN backbones are most likely to be meshes while local backbones are more frequently buses and rings.

If you have mission-critical applications running on your network, you need the high availability a good backbone can give you. In the project opposite, you will analyze your backbone needs by looking at traffic flows. Prepare your data for this analysis by using your network management system. You may also use portable protocol analyzers to capture traffic on specific segments.

Your Backbone

In order to decide what kind of backbone you need, you need to think about both average and maximum traffic levels and also the specific applications that are running on your network.

☐ Think about the number of segments that your devices are distributed on. Think about where servers and mainframes are located. Think about the direction of traffic flow.

• Are there certain segments that contain the most critical data repositories in the network?

• Are they joined by multiport repeaters rather than bridges or routers?

☐ Of the technologies available:

• Which ones do you think are most appropriate for your local backbones?

• Which are most appropriate for your campuses?

• Which are most appropriate for your wide-area connections?

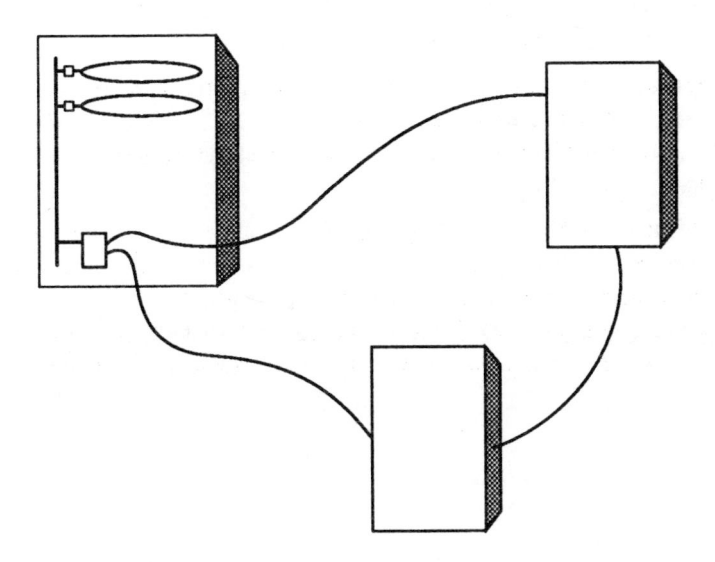

Should You Collapse Your Backbone?

The backbones we discussed on the previous page are all examples of **distributed backbones**: a ring or bus with routers attached to it and networks attached to the routers. Now let's look at a second option—the **collapsed backbone**.

You can "collapse" your network backbone into a single box by using the backplane of your router. If you are using FDDI or one of the high-speed technologies discussed in Chapter 5 for your backplane, this element runs much faster than a distributed backbone of Ethernet or Token Ring. Beyond the speed issue, collapsing your backbone takes the backbone out of the walls where it can be damaged and encloses it in your major infrastructure component: a routing hub, a standalone router or a switch of some kind. You will certainly save money on equipment costs, network management may be easier since fewer components are involved and they are tightly integrated, performance may improve because your LANs are connected directly to the backplane and you may find it easier to segment your servers or mainframes on their own LAN segments. The major disadvantage, of course, is the creation of a single point of failure. The box you collapse your backbone into needs fully redundant components.

Generally, the concentration device—hub, router or switch—gets placed in a central equipment room like a wiring closet. If one closet can't serve the building, you extend the backbone by linking the closets.

Collapsed backbones aren't appropriate for all networks. If long distances are involved, you can't connect all of your users to a single location so you can't collapse your backbone. In addition, if your multiprotocol strategy gives different managers responsibility for different parts of the network, this solution may not be politically palatable.

Collapsing Your Building's Backbones Into a Single Box

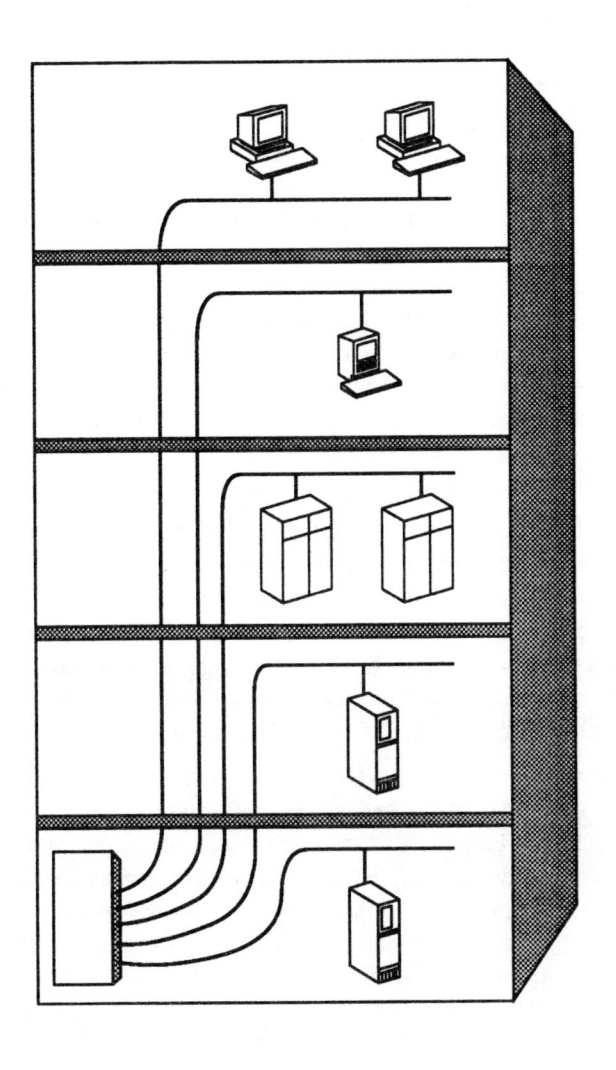

Horrible Case #1: The Campus With Too Many Repeaters

Once upon a time, there was a college with a 12 building campus. In an attempt to save money (you know this story is going to end badly), the MIS staff decided to use only bridges and multiport repeaters for the entire 4,500 device campus. One building—let's call it the Extra-Terrestrial Studies Department (ESD)—has 300 Macintoshes, EtherTalk wiring, 11 servers and a local network administrator with a pervasive feeling of impending doom. The fact that his building is adding 30 new devices a month and all that he has to keep out the barbarian hordes of broadcast storms, chernobyl packets and other problems from all the other buildings on campus is a single bridge might have something to do with this feeling. Our local network administrator can't get the MIS staff to spend money developing a network architecture that protects networks from campus-wide meltdowns (buy routers) but he wants to do what he can to help his local users.

Our admin knows that the network growth has to be managed or faculty and students will not have the reliability they need. Specifically, he needs a stronger firewall connection to the campus backbone, he needs to segment his local users with something more sophisticated than repeaters and he needs to manage traffic to the servers better. How would you improve this network? Cover up this page and work on the illustration opposite before you continue reading. Then compare your solution with what this admin (let's call him Jean-Luc) did.

JL scrounged up some funds and put in an backbone for his building, then bought three bridges and connected the existing networks to the new backbone. He put five servers with building-wide database access needs onto the backbone. He placed the bridges so as to segment the network into approximately equal (by traffic) parts. Without telling MIS, JL reprogrammed the building bridge with extra filters to protect the local LANs from some kinds of global meltdown. He also told the workgroup managers that if they tried to attach additional workstations to the network without getting his blessing, he would unplug the TV in the faculty lounge.

Campus Case

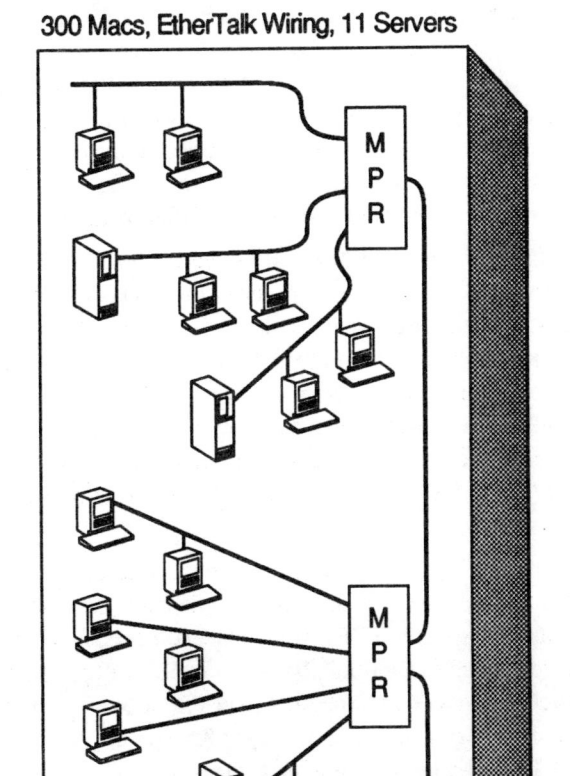

300 Macs, EtherTalk Wiring, 11 Servers

The Evolution of SNA

In Chapter 1, we explored the evolution of SNA from a hierarchical, mainframe architecture through the development of Token Ring and APPN (the New SNA) to the announcement of true multi-architecture distributed computing (the New New SNA). In Chapter 4, we discussed SNA's growing middleware offerings. The IBM Distributed Relational Database Architecture (**DRDA**) brings multi-platform database access to SNA. In order to serve the multi-architecture networking needs of the 1990s, SNA needs to transition to a flat, peer-oriented architecture. The linchpin for the success of this evolution is APPN.

One of the SNA-isms that APPN will eliminate is subarea routing. Subarea routing means that traffic destined for a specific LAN has to go through a specific FEP, making the FEP a potential bottleneck. For greater efficiency, users need to make their connections directly to the host or server application, without having to be routed through a specific FEP—just as users in non-SNA networks do. A user should begin a session by looking up the desired resource—host or server—in a directory (like X.500, StreetTalk, etc.) and then make a direct connection to the resource.

In traditional SNA, you can only make a connection into a subarea through that subarea FEP and you can only make out-of-area connections through specific FEPs. If a connection becomes congested or fails, the application will fail, because the FEP will not automatically recreate the connection through another FEP to keep the user's application alive. (Some network managers have eliminated FEPs and installed Token Rings with remote bridges and routers specifically to improve response time for user applications.) None of this mimics the dynamic rerouting of connections that you learned about in Chapter 3, when dealing with routers.

Before we move on to APPN details, let's look at the larger issue of integrating SNA networks with routed IP backbones and their dynamic bridge/routers. IBM's Data Link Switching (**DLS**) products integrate SDLC with IP by stripping off the SDLC header and replacing it with a TCP/IP header. (Vendors that encapsulate leave the SDLC header intact.)

The New New SNA

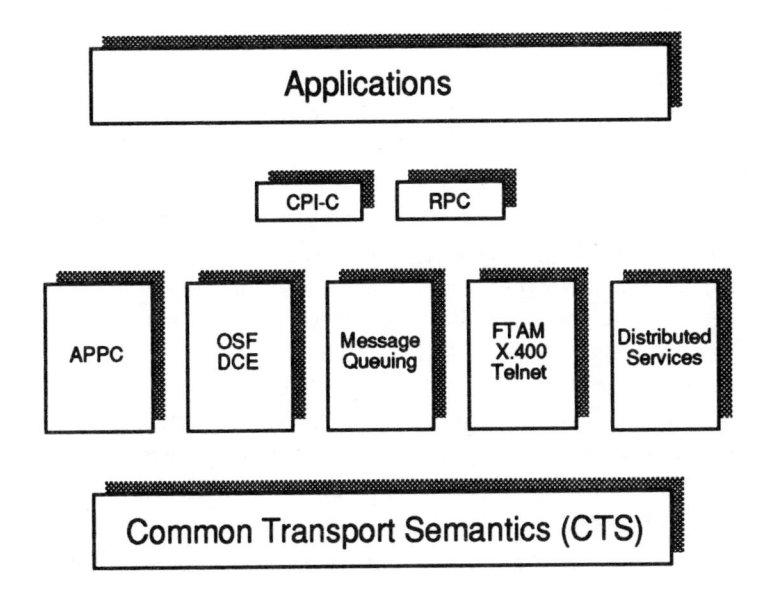

```
┌─────────────────────────────────────────────┐
│               Applications                  │
└─────────────────────────────────────────────┘

              ┌───────┐   ┌─────┐
              │ CPI-C │   │ RPC │
              └───────┘   └─────┘

┌──────┐ ┌──────┐ ┌────────┐ ┌───────┐ ┌───────────┐
│      │ │ OSF  │ │Message │ │ FTAM  │ │Distributed│
│ APPC │ │ DCE  │ │Queuing │ │ X.400 │ │ Services  │
│      │ │      │ │        │ │Telnet │ │           │
└──────┘ └──────┘ └────────┘ └───────┘ └───────────┘

┌─────────────────────────────────────────────┐
│     Common Transport Semantics (CTS)        │
└─────────────────────────────────────────────┘
```

Eliminating Parallel Networks

The cost-saving benefits of combining SNA and routed IP networks are obvious—you may be wasting $250,000 a year per leased line for each "extra" connection. In addition, parallel networks require multiple internetworking infrastructures (bridges, gateways, etc.) and staffs. The challenge is to consolidate your networks while maintaining or improving user service levels. To do this, you need to plan carefully and understand the technical differences between SNA and traditional LAN traffic.

The first place you may stub your toe is the timing constraints of SNA sessions. If an SDLC session stays idle for more than about 7 seconds, the session gets dropped. In a LAN environment this would be laughable but think about how SDLC developed: cluster controllers with dedicated links to users and FEPs. This protocol was not designed to deal with shared bandwidth. Unless you migrate your SNA network to Token Ring, add conversion devices or use poll spoofing, your SNA users will notice big changes in the new integrated network. Performance problems with timeouts are particularly prevalent in international connections.

What you really need is a way to prioritize traffic in your WAN so that time-sensitive traffic like SNA gets priority over traffic that can wait. In SNA, Class of Service (**COS**) allows you to set priority levels for traffic types, so you can ensure that your mission-critical applications keep running regardless of congestion. You could also prioritize based on the type of receiving device, so host-destined sessions could get higher priorities. Several router vendors are offering COS-like priority to reduce SNA timeouts. Some performance measures say that OSPF (used with IP) can discover a new route around a failure in three seconds. This suggests that an OSPF IP routed backbone can serve the session performance needs of SNA users.

In dealing with SNA timeout problems, the other alternative is to create a backbone that's so fast even SNA can't time out. Managers who take the second path will find inspiration in the technologies of Chapter 5.

An SNA Session That Crosses an IP WAN

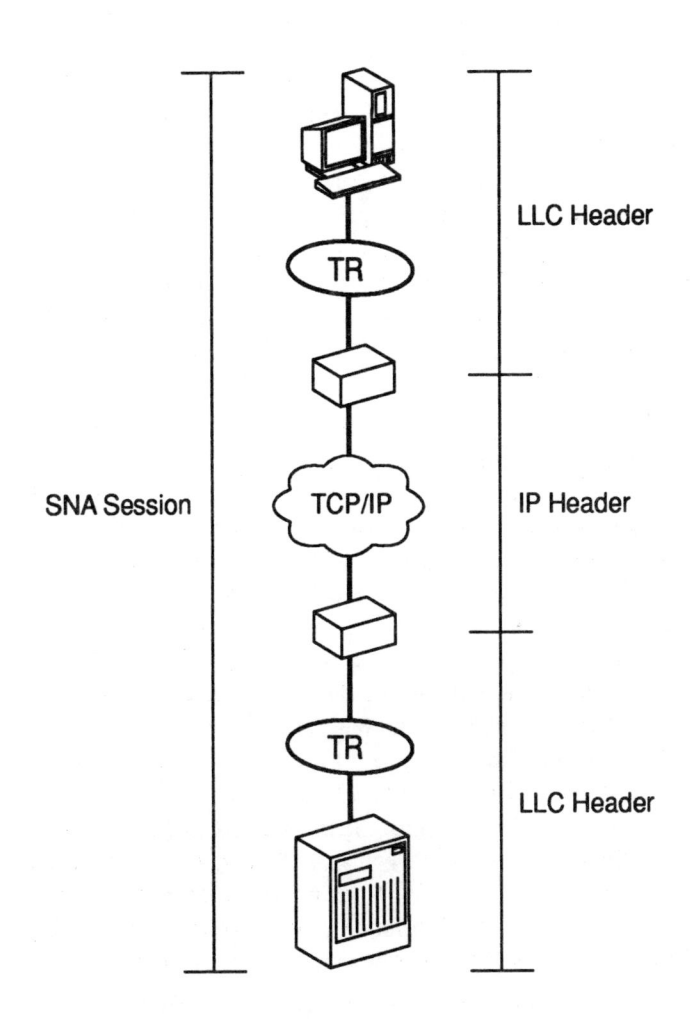

Working With APPN

APPN is one way to allow bridge/router vendors to integrate SNA traffic onto existing routed backbones carrying IPX and IP packets. The essential component of an APPN network is **Network Node** (NN) software. These NNs route traffic and maintain directories of End Nodes (desktops, servers, hosts, etc.). Router vendors are integrating NN software into their devices, including board-level products integrated into muxes and switches. VTAM Version 4 enables IBM hosts to act as NNs. Unfortunately, APPN routing is not dynamic enough to preserve sessions when a link fails or becomes congested. One weakness of APPN is that it only supports interactions using LU 6.2/APPC. In future, it will also support other native SNA session types. Below APPN you need specific APIs like LU 6.2's CPI-C (Common Programming Interface-Communications), as well as RPCs, MQM and other middleware APIs.

APPI, supported by the APPI Forum, supports APPN End Nodes but encapsulates these packets in IP for WAN transport. The routers that link APPN to the IP backbone are called Open Network Nodes (ONN). APPI is aimed at networks that already use IP for their internet backbone and want to integrate APPN End Nodes into the same structure. Under APPI, APPN and IP coexist and share the same infrastructure. In APPI, the **Open Network Nodes** communicate with End Nodes using LU6.2. APPI has a distributed directory service, just like APPN, where certain routers are responsible for directory service. When an ONN receives a connection request to an unknown network, it requests directory assistance from the local designated directory server. In Stage 2 of APPI, ONNs will get SNA intermediate routing and an SNMP MIB. APPI differs from APPN in that APPI provides a mechanism for APPI traffic to travel alongside IP traffic on the same network paths. Because APPI offers COS priorities for congestion control, SNA/APPN traffic gets the priority treatment it needs to perform well.

The New New SNA, under either APPN or APPI, should allow you to run your SNA applications over TCP/IP transport and vice versa.

The APPI ONNs

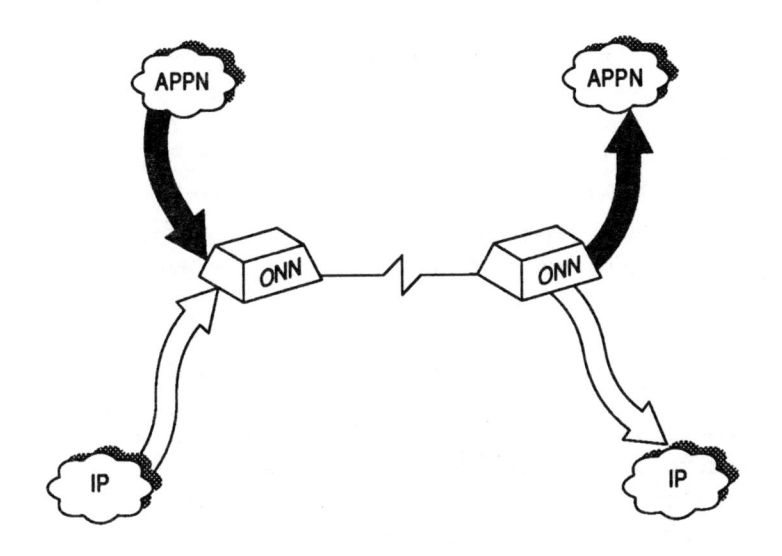

TCP/IP and OSI

Although GOSIP has had an impact on the OSI market, sales have continued to be slow compared to older architectures, primarily the TCP/IP stack. The major arguments in favor of TCP/IP can be distilled into excellent business sense—it has a track record; it works—but the future clearly belongs to international standards and multi-protocol networking. Since TCP/IP needs to interoperate with international OSI networks, and we need to prepare migration plans for an eventual phase-out of TCP/IP protocols, let's survey the existing protocols and architecture strategies that will make this transition easier.

The Internet itself is taking advantage of OSI development work in two key areas: addressing and routing. IP is running out of available Internet addresses and the IETF has proposed solving this problem by switching to OSI addressing, with effectively unlimited capacity. TCP/IP networks are also using the OSI IS/IS routing protocol (Chapter 3), along with OSPF, to replace RIP. The IETF is considering adding IS/IS to the list of protocol options for the Internet because it is a robust link state protocol. Integrated IS/IS, which consolidates routing information from multiple protocols in the same network, is another bridge between TCP/IP users and the OSI world.

In the network management area, Common Management Interface Protocol Over TCP/IP (**CMOT**) is a version of CMIP designed specifically for TCP/IP environments. It hasn't enjoyed much market success yet, because of the proliferation of SNMP in these networks. It will undoubtedly become more popular as migration accelerates. SNMP over OSI protocols is also a likely development.

Add Some OSI To Your Network

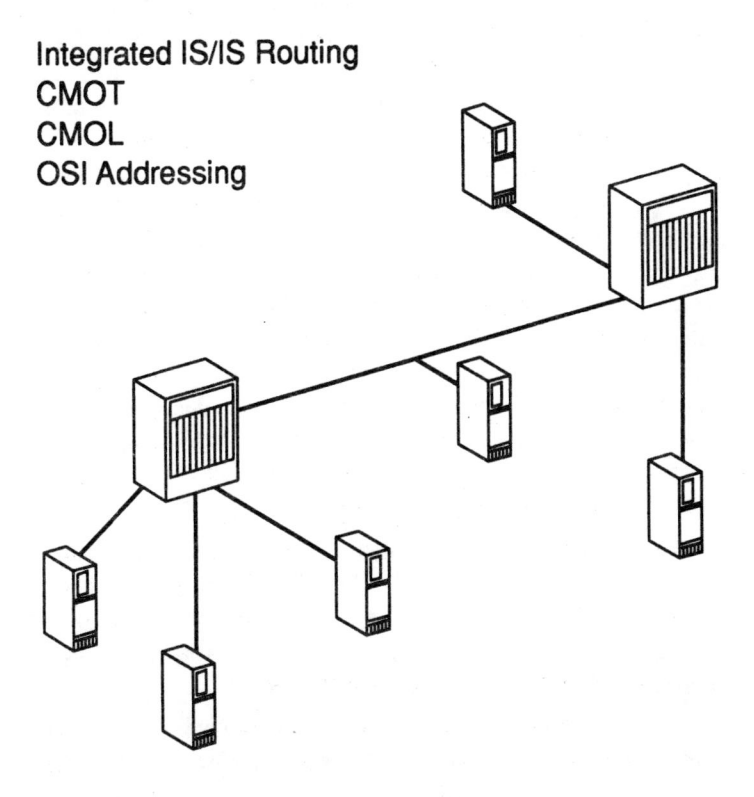

Integrated IS/IS Routing
CMOT
CMOL
OSI Addressing

The Skinny Stack Proposal

The Corporation for Open Systems (COS), which promotes standards development in North America, has proposed a **skinny stack** to help make it easier for TCP/IP networks to migrate to OSI. Because it is an international standard, the OSI protocols contain many more options than the average U.S. network manager needs. Deleting some of the options will delete a lot of complexity (and overhead) and make an OSI stack that can run as efficiently as TCP/IP. Skinny OSI slims down in Layers 5 and 6. You get the critical OSI advantages of global addressing and robust routing at Layers 3 and 4 while losing presentation and session services, and FTAM and ROSE at the Application Layer. The thinned application layer has a transport API to link it to Layer 4. This means that you can run TCP/IP applications over the more robust OSI transport infrastructure. Database request/response is an example of a response critical application that would benefit from this approach. Client/server applications and groupware, as they become more common as data handling strategies, increase the amount of request/response traffic on the network.

The skinny stack can handle applications using UNIX Sockets and the X/Open Transport Interface (XTI). The original skinny stack concept came from work done by the ANSI X3H3.6 committee, working on the X Window interface. Applications developers can work more quickly without the complexity inherent in Layers 5 and 6.

The Common Management Interface Protocol Over Logical Link (CMOL) protocol was suggested for "short stacks" with minimal software needs over the Data Link Layer. Applications with simple routing and minimal error recovery, like remote banking transactions, for example, are good candidates for CMOL management.

Skinny OSI Stack

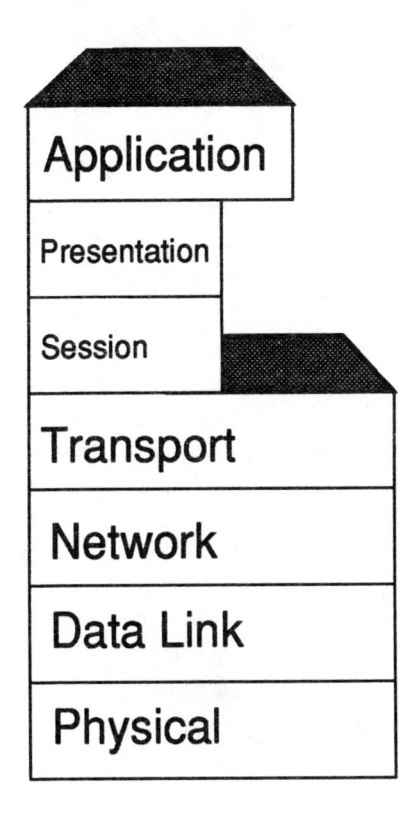

| Application |
| Presentation |
| Session |
| Transport |
| Network |
| Data Link |
| Physical |

DEC Advantage Networks

Let's take a look at an OSI-conforming architecture called DECnet/OSI, now being used as glue for multi-architecture distributed computing. The entire architecture, including DECnet/OSI, APIs, gateways and other software, is now called Advantage Networks.

The major advance in DECnet/OSI comes from robust OSI addressing and routing protocols. For example, DECnet Phase IV routing has a maximum of 64,000 addresses per network while OSI addressing will give you over 280 trillion addresses per network. Integrated IS/IS routing gives the networks link state routing. (Routers must be migrated to the new software to avoid problems associated with different routing protocols).

Advantage Networks includes three main "towers"—DECnet, OSI and TCP/IP—with programming interfaces to link them. This means that applications (above the towers) should eventually be able to access information on any network regardless of the transport. For instance, look at the FTP–FTAM and VMS–FTAM gateways. **Pathworks**, the DEC NOS, will be the vehicle for much of the interoperability at the server level, allowing a variety of desktops to connect to servers using VMS, Ultrix (DEC's UNIX version) and OS/2. The new version of Pathworks includes native NetWare filing and printing services for tighter integration with NetWare networks.

APIs are the main strategy for speeding up application development and making it possible for applications to run over a variety of transport. All the APIs fall under Network Application Support (**NAS**), an architecture for efficient application development. NAS includes some APIs that work with specific towers as well as generic APIs like RPCs. Applications use the Distributed Naming Service (DNS, similar in function and identical in acronym to the Internet's Domain Name Service) as their global directory. The Distributed Timing Service (DTS) and Concert Multi-thread Architecture (CMA) facilitate parallel processing by synchronizing time stamps and insuring that as tasks are distributed throughout the network, they are executed in the proper order. DEC developed Distributed Systems Security Architecture (DSSA) for authentication and encryption.

Advantage Network Towers

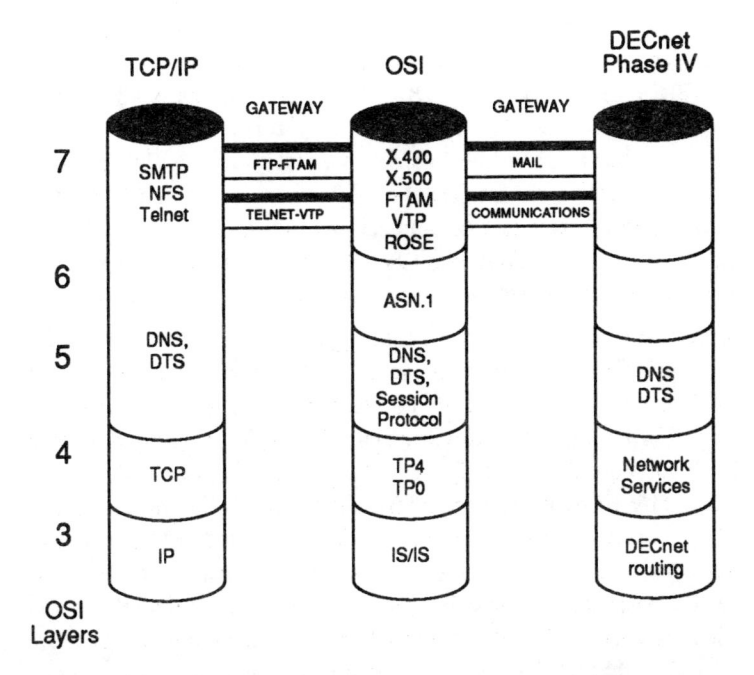

OSI Layers	TCP/IP		OSI		DECnet Phase IV
		GATEWAY		GATEWAY	
7	SMTP, NFS, Telnet	FTP-FTAM / TELNET-VTP	X.400, X.500, FTAM, VTP, ROSE	MAIL / COMMUNICATIONS	
6			ASN.1		
5	DNS, DTS		DNS, DTS, Session Protocol		DNS, DTS
4	TCP		TP4, TP0		Network Services
3	IP		IS/IS		DECnet routing

Multiple Towers and Distributed Applications

Advantage Networks also includes more powerful SNA gateways for improved integration with New SNA networks. By making an attached DECnet network look like an SNA subarea to the IBM host, attached 3270 users can make connections to the DECnet network as easily as if it were an SNA network and they can also print ASCII characters on an IBM printer. Advantage Networks plans to add an X.400–SMTP gateway connecting the OSI and TCP/IP towers and another gateway linking Telnet to OSI's VTP (Virtual Terminal Protocol). The Transport Layer connection for the OSI and TCP towers is XTI and RFC1006, which allows existing OSI applications to run on top of TCP. The multi-protocol path from one tower to another is called a particular connection's **tower set**. Multi-protocol routers use Integrated IS/IS.

Application integration is the ultimate goal of all the other types of integration; users need to be able to get to the information they need to do their jobs. One of the most important tools for this integration is the Distributed Computing Environment (DCE) produced by the Open Software Foundation (OSF) we first mentioned in Chapter 4. DCE is being offered by many vendors (including DEC) who are part of the OSF consortium. DCE is available with OSF/1 and IBM's AIX, two versions of UNIX, and there are new versions that work with TCP. DCE's basic services include a global name service, a time stamp service, various RPCs and a **threads** facility. A global time stamp is required so that all the network's nodes can synchronize their internal clocks and perform functions at the proper time. Threads allow an application to execute multiple functions simultaneously, for example, an I/O operation with a database fetch. On top of these basic services, DCE has options for a distributed file system and distributed printing.

DCE Architecture

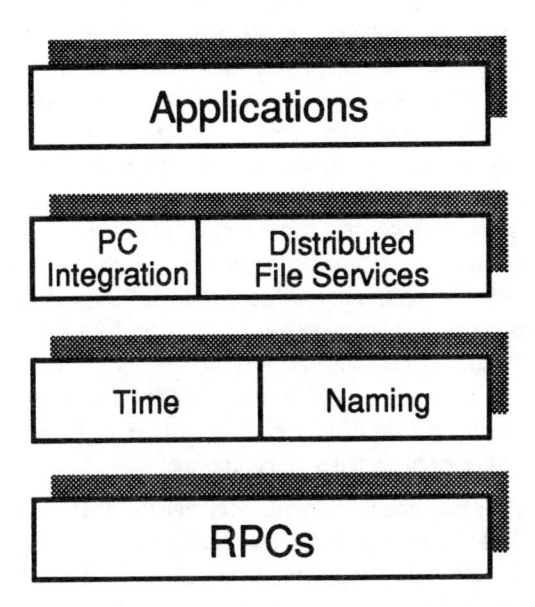

Applications

PC Integration	Distributed File Services

Time	Naming

RPCs

OS and Transport (+ Threads)

Integrating Wireless Networks

While most LANs continue to be wired, there is a growing need for wireless networks. By 1998, wireless LANs will probably account for 20% of all new LAN shipments. User applications for wireless LANs are "nomadic" applications like express package delivery, shipping and receiving, warehouse and other situations where a worker has to move through the environment, carrying a very lightweight, portable access device. These LANs are also useful in hazardous environments, where wire can cause sparks and fire danger, and areas that would not be cost-effective to wire, like some remote portions of the building. Wireless networks are frequently infrared, for line-of-sight applications, and radio frequency, for building-wide or floor-wide use. Some network managers are using wireless LANs to bridge two wired infrastructures, bypassing the switched telephone system. Retailers such as K-Mart are using wireless LANs for roving inventory control, with workers who can walk the aisles recording and making enquiries. Most wireless LANs are connected to the corporate, wired network.

Wireless LANs may end up impacting consumers in retail sales before they make a decisive impact on more traditional office applications. For example, the Raley's supermarket chain in Northern California uses two different kinds of integrated wireless LANs with their intelligent shopping carts. Each cart carries a flat panel display connected to a infrared location network and a radio frequency (RF) product information network. The infrared sensors on the cart communicate with overhead network nodes and give you a constantly updated store map with your current location. If you need to find a specific item, the control panel communicates via the RF network to tell you exactly where the item is relative to where you currently are. This wireless network is much more sophisticated than we have space to cover here. The wireless networks are connected to the headquarters, wired network via a dialup router (Chapter 3). In the Raley's case, the router provides integration for the two network types. Other solutions include bridges, modems and specialized convertors.

The IEEE 802.11 subcommittee is working on a Physical and MAC Layer standard but obviously work is not as far advanced as the older wired standards. To allow multiple services to coexist, most networks use **spread spectrum** technology in which the network connection is spread over several frequency bands, in a pre-arranged pattern.

Integrating Wireless LANs

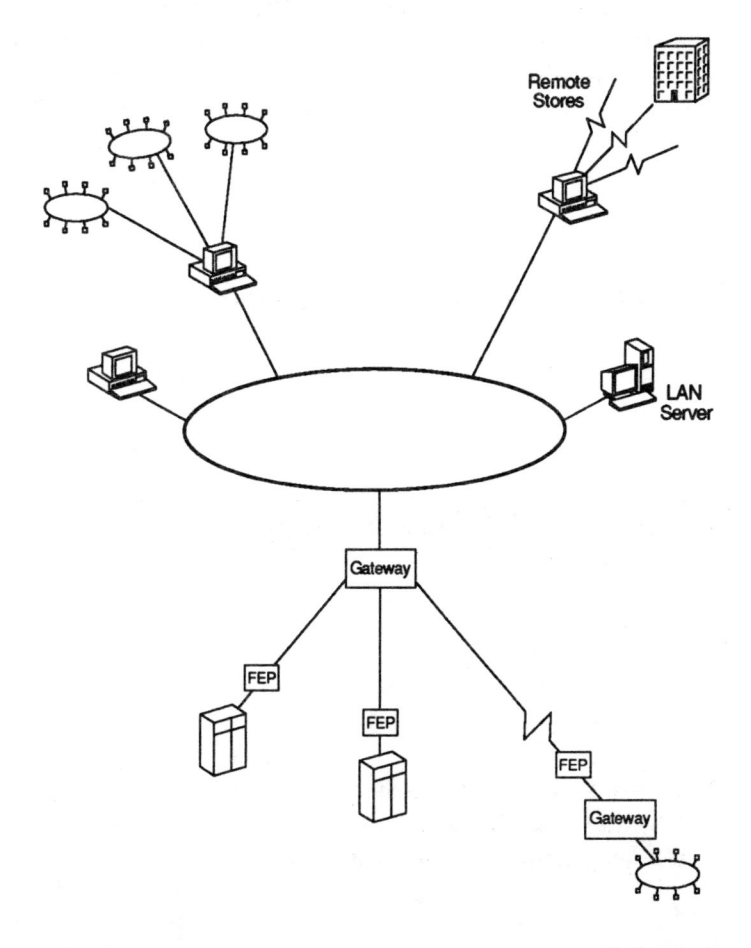

This network manager has been migrating the corporate network from mainframe based architecture to a distributed Token Ring architecture while he simultaneously moves some applications to servers. You see here the transition architecture. Remote stores use local wireless LANs and connect to the corporate backbone through the remote bridge in the upper right corner.

Developing a Strategy

In keeping with the overall movement to integrating functions at the board level into hubs, both conversion and encapsulation are becoming available as hub add-ons. The strategy saves the cost of standalone devices; the performance impact varies. In addition, network managers are consolidating parallel SNA and IP networks onto single backbones.

Work on this checklist to help develop a personalized strategy for your network:

☐ What protocol stacks are you currently using?

☐ With respect to your backbone, can you improve the topology? Can you simplify?

☐ Do you have parallel connections that you could amalgamate? Where are they? (Spend time planning before you shop. In particular, get performance data on both networks.)

- ☐ What technologies can you investigate to improve the efficiency of your multi-protocol infrastructure?
  - to improve speed
  - to improve security

- ☐ What software infrastructure do you need to support multi-protocol applications access using your protocols?

- ☐ Should you collapse part or all of your backbone? What are the tradeoffs for your specific network?

- ☐ What hardware and software should you consider to help tighten security as you consolidate your network and make information more accessible to legitimate users?

- ☐ Are your local network administrators asking you for money and being turned away? Are your local administrators doing things that you only find out about later? (This is a warning sign to improve communication.)

Perhaps a campus-wide bake sale or Network Relief benefit concert would embarrass the CFO into investing in the tools that your end users need to better serve customers—the ultimate reason for your business existence.

Summary

- Multi-protocol networking primarily involves TCP/IP, SNA, AppleTalk, DECnet and Novell networks.
- Multi-protocol networking can use tunnelling, encapsulation, conversion, NOSs, middleware or gateways. A distributed computing architecture provides the best framework for this kind of networking
- Backbones carry LAN–LAN traffic. Using the proper technology and topology is critical. You can collapse your backbone into a single box.
- The most important component of SNA migration is APPN.
- APPI is competing for acceptance in mixed SNA/IP environments.
- The skinny stack proposal and DEC Advantage Networks are two strategies for integrating OSI into your current network design.
- Wireless networks are becoming more popular and can be integrated into wired infrastructures, using async routers and specialized converters.

Chapter 6 – Review

1. Name the most common architectures involved in multi-protocol networks.
2. List the components of the New SNA. What added components comprise the New New SNA?
3. Name two primary ways to link a pure SNA network to a token ring network: _____ and _____.
4. If we both have token ring networks and we need to communicate via a TCP/IP-based wide-area network, what is our best interoperability strategy? Why?
5. If the backbone fails, what happens to individual networks? What applications are most impacted?

BACKBONES AND MULTI-PROTOCOL INTERNETS

6. List 2 new **technologies** that can be used as backbones for campus networks. For each technology come up with at least 2 reasons why this technology is appropriate for campuses.
7. List 2 **technologies** that are currently used as risers and other backbones in multi-story buildings? Why are these technologies popular in this application?
8. What **topologies** are popular for intra-building backbones?
9. What **topologies** are popular for campus backbones?
10. Do specific topologies seem to work best for multi-protocol internetworks? Which ones? **Why**?
11. What business issues seem to be spurring interest in collapsed backbones?
12. What kinds of companies would be most helped by collapsed backbones? Are you one of them? **Why**?
13. List at least 2 protocols that have been developed as part of the integration of TCP/IP and OSI networking? What are their functions?
14. Skinny stacks delete functionality at which layers?
15. OSI networks have (more/less) available addresses than IP?
16. Architectures in Advantage Networks are called _____.
17. What is a thread and how does it impact distributed computing?
18. OSF developed the _____ architecture for distributed computing.
19. ONNs integrate _____ and _____ protocols.
20. ONN was developed by the _____ Forum.
21. Two strategies for avoiding SNA timeouts are _____ and _____.
22. List 2 applications for an integrated wired/wireless network.

Key Words

The words and phrases highlighted in **bold** represent key concepts in this chapter. Please take the time now to write down your definitions of these terms, using the list below and additional paper if needed. Then compare your efforts to the training text. This is an excellent way for you to determine weak points in the breadth and depth of your understanding of this chapter.

risers

distributed backbones

collapsed backbone

DRDA

DLS

COS

Network Node

Open Network Node

CMOT

skinny stack

pathworks

NAS

tower set

threads

spread spectrum

7
Le Quiz

The comprehensive final exam for this Internetworking course is a crossword puzzle. Don't panic! Crossword puzzles can be great fun.

If you haven't completed a puzzle in a while, keep these hints in mind:

- Numbers are written out in words.
- Punctuation (dashes, for example) is ignored.
- If you think you have one answer figured out but it seems to preclude one or more other answers (pqw can't be an OSI Layer, can it?), think about the questions again. Sometimes you will see another way of approaching the question.
- Most importantly, go through the puzzle in its entirety once and fill in all the "easy" answers before you try the harder questions.

Enjoy!

Advanced Internetworking Puzzle

Down

2. Link state routing protocol
3. Autonomous system
4. Physical unit
5. SONET in Europe
6. They say HELLO to routers (pl.)
7. Strategy for speeding application development
8. Bridging in IBM networks
12. A collection of networks
15. Electronics trade organization
17. CCITT's parent's parent
18. Can do bridging and routing
20. Spanning tree prevents this
21. Collection of networks
22. Router, in OSI terminology
23. Technology touted to solve all problems (pl.)
24. Older border router protocol
26. Nautical multiprotocol method
30. ISDN's 23b+d
31. 802.6: D_ _ _
32. Standards group: A_ _ _

Across

1. You can do this to your backbone
7. Autonomous system
9. Bad topologies put you in the _____
10. Chapter 5 technologies get good _____
11. Network managers need _____ vacations
13. Used in data centers
14. _____ relay
16. Hang out at IEEE meetings

LE QUIZ

17. OS used as a NOS
19. ATM layer that interfaces higher layers
21. Her failures are more public than your netman staff's
23. APPN reduces sub-_____ routing
25. DOS is one
26. High-speed synchronous network technology
27. Network Layer protocol
28. Unroutable protocol
29. New SNA component
31. Congestion control strategy
33. OSI routing: I _ / _ _
34. Link states shared with these routers

See *Appendix A* for the solution to the puzzle.

Appendix A: Answer Keys

Chapter 0

1. b
2. a
3. c
4. c
5. d
6. b
7. Users complain about response time
8. d
9. c. An IP router will not bridge AppleTalk nor can it route it.
10. a
11. c
12. b
13. a
14. c
15. c

16. b
17. d

Chapter 2

Transparent Bridges:
> bridge 16 is the root because it has the lowest number ID; bridge 21 will never hear a configuration message from bridges 50 and 25 because they will hear bridge 16's message passed on by bridges 18 and 21 and will decide that they are not the root.

Let's build a spanning tree:
> the following bridges have all ports in the tree: 1, 2, 3, 10, 7, 5 and 6. The following bridges have no ports in the tree: 4, 8, 9 and 11. B1 is the root. It's message is 1, 0, 1. If bridge 4 fails, nothing will happen; it isn't in the active tree. If bridges 7 or 3 fail, bridge 4 will put its ports into forwarding mode.

1. RI field includes SR paths
2. The multicast bit in the source address is set
3. All route discovery
4. Routes age; the bridge hop limit of seven; must be manually configured; explorers eat up WAN bandwidth
5. Time delay while a new ST is created; filtering may no longer be appropriate after the transparent bridge reconfigures; congestion can cripple ST
6. LLC
7. Not
8. Reasons to trade: reliability, segmentation, traffic management
   Reasons to upgrade: easy migration, cheaper migration, flexibility
9. You need conversion, not passthrough
10. Local spoofing
11. Uniform; workgroup
12. SR-TB
13. Root, lowest

APPENDIX A: ANSWER KEYS

14. Forwarding
15. Seven
16. Size of the RI field; No or the overall frame size would increase
17. WAN

Chapter 3

1. A/b, B/a, C/e, D/d, E/c, F/g, G/f
2. Faster convergence, less inter-router traffic, more accurate routing information, no hop count limit
3. Exterior Gateway Protocol
4. If the servers include gateway software, they are converting from one packet type to another. They could also have router (level 1) software resident on the server. The NOS itself is not a router and does not communicate with other routers.
5. Border Gateway Protocol
7. If you use both protocols you need to redistribute routing information, standardize on one or the other or run both protocols simultaneously.
8. Local traffic will reach its destination but your network has partitioned from the rest of the internet so you cannot make connections through the border router.
9. When a link comes up or down, when a cost changes, regularly as a keepalive, when routers receive a new neighbor HELLO.
10. No; Yes
11. Report link failure
12. One address for every connection; a two port device has two connections
13. Traffic, administrative, community of interest (to apply global commands).
14. AURP
15. Broadcast updates only when changes occur.
16. RIP (This chapter mentions RIP with IPX.)

17. No, you need an SDLC to 802.2 converter
18. No, it slows convergence. It does prevent routing loops and rapid oscillations.
19. Link
20. Adjacency
21. Domains, ASs. Confederation
22. Global timing, sequence numbers
23. Not recommended. Integrated IS/IS is designed for IP and OSI, not SNA.
24. Protocols are added, deleted, upgraded, and cause problems separately. Each protocol must discover routing information on its own and use up more bandwidth with duplicate routing updates.
25. 4, 5, communications controllers, hosts
26. Dialup
27. 256 (2^8)

Chapter 4

1. Layer 5, 6, 7
2. NetWare, VINES, LAN Server, LAN Manager
3. NetWare
4. First in the market place
5. NetWare Lite or LANtastic because you don't need sophisticated features
6. NetWare 4.0 or VINES
7. NOSs are developing agents to interoperate with each other
8. No. Agents exist that will allow a Netware Manager to communicate with a VI NES server device.
9. Independent
10. Client/server
11. Lower cost platforms, lower cost server platforms; separate elements can evolve, be maintained and managed more easily; computing power is distributed, user response improves etc.

APPENDIX A: ANSWER KEYS

12. Back end, front end
13. LAN Server
14. A Server
15. NetWare advantages: Market dominance, different versions for different sized networks, especially good for smaller networks. Advantages of VINES based on UNIX platform; particularly advantageous for large heterogeneous networks; robust directory service
16. UNIX
17. VINES, UNIX
18. Asymmetrical
19. Software layer between the transport and the applications, it acts as a meta-API to speed application development and improve application portability.
20. No. No. Yes. Yes. No. Yes. Yes. Yes. No
21. No. Too small and unsophisticated
22. Yes. Application portability becomes important in this network.

Chapter 5

2. DQDB, SMDS, Frame Relay.
3. It ensures fairness; traffic from multiple sources can be separately billed; it can carry multiple traffic types (at the MAC layer).
4. SONET
5. DQDB
6. ANSI, CCITT, CCITT (they are both members of the I.xx family). Other forums and groups are contributing but they are not official standards organizations.
7. 802.6 DQDB
8. B
9. PA
10. Isochronous traffic gets PA slots and data queues up on a first come, first served basis. See the text for details.
11. ATM, SONET, DQDB, ISDN. SONET is just a physical fabric, the

others are MACs. SMDS and FR can't carry voice/video.
12. CLP and PTI
13. 53 octets, 5
14. ATM, Frame Relay. Connection oriented services can guarantee data delivery without adding any additional software. They generally require more overhead.
15. Synchronous optical network.
16. Yes. SONET is a physical layer technology, so it treats bits only as bits. It has ways of integrating both voice/video and data into payloads. See Your Pocket SONET/ATM Glossary.
17. Section, line and path. Path is managed by CPE, Section is in repeaters and line is in muxes.
18. SDH, 155.5
19. Yes. SONET is a physical fabric that can carry almost anything. Frame Relay is a MAC.
20. In the long term, possibly. ATM can carry voice and video, which Frame Relay can't. But Frame Relay does not require such high speeds as ATM does in order to be effective as a business solution. Also ATM is very costly in overhead. Management of ATM is not well developed yet.
21. SONET, they are both ANSI standards.
22. SMDS
23. T carrier can fit inside SONET payloads and is being used as a low speed rollout for SMDS, ATM, and other MACs.
24. It's not efficient at speeds under 35 Mbps.
25. The ATM layer (that wasn't hard to remember!).

Chapter 6

1. SNA, DECnet, TCP/IP
2. LU 6.2, APPC, APPN. Middleware, multi-protocol transport

APPENDIX A: ANSWER KEYS

3. Tunnelling, conversion
4. Tunnelling. Conversion not needed because both endpoints are Token Ring.
5. Individual networks can transport local traffic only. Applications that make connections to databases off the local net.
6. SONET, DQDB, ATM, FDDI. You need high speed and reliability.
7. Ethernet, 16 Mbps Token Ring, FDDI. Inexpensive relatively high bandwidth, well known technologies.
8. Star/bus, ring
9. Ring, mesh
10. If gateways are needed, stars work well, as do meshes
11. Saving money on wiring. Keeping the backbone safe from damage, making the backbone more manageable lower cost also. Adding new technologies without adding a new backbone.
12. Companies with an internet mostly within a building or campus of buildings, companies who need to keep netman staff low, companies without an existing routed backbone.
13. CMOT, CMOL (network management), Integrated IS/IS (routing), OSI addressing for the Internet
14. 5 and 6
15. More
16. Towers
17. Threads specify a path of computations. With distributed computing, you have to ensure that computations occur in order.
18. DCE
19. IP, SNA/APPN
20. APPI
21. Class of service and other priorities, very fast backbones
22. Wireless segments in retail outlets, warehouses, shipping/receiving docks, dangerous environments, remote corners of a building, nomadic users

Chapter 7

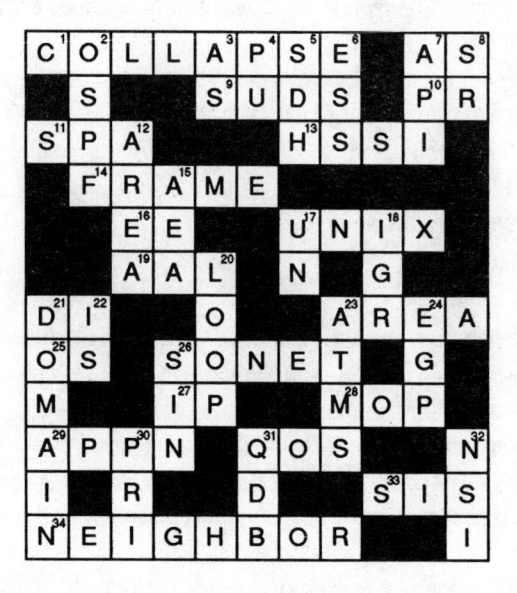

Appendix B: Publications, Conferences & Additional Reading

Publications

If you are not already receiving these publications, call and request a sample copy or visit your local technical bookstore:

Business Communications Review
Hinsdale, IL (800) 227-1234

Communications Week (weekly news)
Manhasset, NY (516) 562-5530

LAN (monthly)
San Francisco, CA (415) 905-2200

LAN Computing (monthly)
Horsham, PA

LAN Times
San Mateo, CA (415) 513-6800

Network Computing (monthly)
Manhasset, NY (516) 562-5071

Networking Management (monthly)
Westford, MA (508) 692-0700

Network World (weekly news)
Framingham, MA (508) 875-6400

In addition, *LAN Technology Magazine* focuses on the needs of systems integrators.

Conferences

There are dozens of good networking conferences every year, in the U.S. and abroad. The shows that focus most heavily on internetworking are the two Interop shows: on the west coast (San Francisco Bay Area) in October and in the District of Columbia area in April. Registration information is available at (415) 941-3399. NetWorld in Boston (Spring) and Dallas (Fall) are also excellent sources of ready-to-buy equipment information. Registration information is available through the Blenheim Group (201) 569-8542.

Additional Reading

For an in-depth, technical treatment of bridging and routing, I highly recommend Radia Perlman's (the mother of spanning tree) *Interconnections: Bridges and Routers*. For those of an engineering bent, Radia is a delight. One strong caveat for business readers: this author is very literate and articulate **for an engineer**. If plowing through 20 pages of tough technical explanations and then being told "Well, none of this stuff exists in products, but maybe it will some day and it's an interesting experiment if someone ever decides to do it" makes you livid over your wasted time and energy, or if you can't stomach naming your servers FOO, or if the j th instance of variable v makes you run screaming from the room, don't buy this book.

About The Author

Victoria Marney-Petix develops and delivers both live and computer-based training programs on network technology and management as Chief Consultant of Marpet Technical Services. In addition to local area networks and internetworking, her course list includes an in-depth look at networking architectures, a course on TCP/IP, an in-depth look at network management strategies and products, a course on ISDN and a two-day seminar on high-speed networking options. She teaches at San Francisco State University Extension and the University of California Santa Cruz Extension.

Victoria also consults with vendors in the U.S. and Europe that are developing new network products and services, especially internet products, and with users who are managing complex internets.

Victoria's first book, *Networking and Data Communication* (1986, Prentice-Hall/Reston), received rave reviews in library publications, including *ONLINE/Database magazine*: "I found myself so absorbed that I read the book in one sitting!...one of the best explanations of local area networks written to date." Her second book, *Client/Server Computing*, was published in 1990. *Mastering Internetworking* (1992) was praised in *Data Communications*, *Network World* and *Computer Books Review* for readability and usefulness.

Victoria has hosted several video training programs, most recently *Intro to LANs* and *Selling the Next Workstation*. In her non-networking life, Victoria is the producer/host of *Carrot Talk*, a weekly cable TV show focusing on care, behavior and training of pet rabbits.

You may contact the author directly at:
Marpet Technical Services
PO Box 2275
Fremont, CA 94536
(510) 792-9204

If you have comments on this book, please communicate with us (rather than the author) at **Numidia Press** by using the Comments form. We appreciate your feedback!

Comments

Title: **Mastering Advanced Internetworking**

Where did you buy this book?

- ❒ mail order
- ❒ bookstore (name) _____
- ❒ employer (name) _____
- ❒ training course _____
- ❒ other (where?) _____

I'd like you to know that: (tell us where we goofed, did a great job, could make improvements, left something out, etc.)

_____
_____
_____
_____
_____

Tell us about yourself. Your name/address/phone is useful if we don't understand and need to call you to clarify, but you can remain incognito if you prefer. Your job title or function will help us to understand what kind of reader the problem impacts and this is important to us. An industry is equally helpful.

_____
_____
_____

We appreciate all your help in making the next edition of this book even better than the present one. Thank you!

Numidia Press • P.O. Box 2281 • Fremont, CA 94536
Phone (510) 790-1199 • Fax (510) 797-5053

Fold here, staple or tape, stamp and mail

Place
Stamp
Here

Numidia Press
P.O. Box 2281
Fremont, CA 94536

Order Form

Please send me the books in the Self-Paced Learning Series:

_____ copies of *Mastering Internetworking* (**$24.95**)

_____ copies of *Mastering Advanced Internetworking* (**$24.95**)

_____ copies of *Mastering Network Management* (6/93) (**$24.95**)

_____ copies of *Mastering LAN Enabling Technologies* (6/93) (**$24.95**)

_____ Total number of books @ $24.95 each

_____ copies of *Alphabet Soup: Networking and Data Comm Acronyms* (**$8.95**)

$_____ Subtotal

$_____ CA addresses add $1.95 sales tax per book in Self-Paced Series and $.75 per *Alphabet Soup*

$_____ Shipping (book rate: $1.50/book, air mail: $2.50/book)

$_____ Amount enclosed

Discounts available on quantity & pre-pub orders!

Name _____

Company/Title _____

Address _____

City _____ State _____ Zip _____

Full money-back guarantee!

Please make check payable to

Numidia Press
P.O. Box 2281
Fremont, CA 94536
(510) 790-1199

❑ Please send me a catalog of books and videos available from Numidia Press

Fold here, staple or tape, stamp and mail

Place
Stamp
Here

Numidia Press
P.O. Box 2281
Fremont, CA 94536

Cut Here

New For Spring!

Alphabet Soup: Networking and Data Comm Acronyms and their Meanings

Julie Weiss $8.95

In handy pocket form, this is the complete compendium of every acronym you're likely to encounter as you buy, sell, manage or work with a network. Every acronym has a definition—no complex tutorials, just the facts!

Pocket-sized format means you can bring this book everywhere—your essential translator in the world of networking.

Order this new release and pay for it before May 1 and get a 20% discount!

New for Summer!

The Self-Paced Learning Series: Mastering Network Management

Ellen Brigham and V. C. Marney-Petix $24.95

An in-depth look at LAN and internet management, including the tools you need, the procedures you need to follow and the protocols to investigate. The focus is on Ethernet, Token Ring, FDDI, TCP/IP, IPX/NetWare and other common network types.

Numidia Press
PO Box 2281
Fremont CA 94536
510 790-1199

Index

Numerics
802.1 .... 10, 24
802.11 154
802.2, see LLC
802.9 114

A
adjacency 50
Advanced Peer to Peer Networking see APPN
Advantage Networks ... 16, 150, 152
advertisements 50
all paths explorer frame 30, 32
ANSI 108, 122, 148
API 76, 86, 94, 150
APPC 14, 144
APPI 14, 144
APPI Forum 144
AppleShare 76, 80
AppleTalk 16, 68, 80, 84, 132
APPN 14, 64, 140, 144
areas 50, 55, 56, 58
ARPAnet 18
Asynchronous Transfer Mode, see ATM
ATM 100, 102, 110, 112, 114, 118, 120, 122, 123, 126
ATM Adaptation Layer (AAL). 112
ATM Forum 112
AURP 68
autonomous systems 50

B
backbones 38, 40, 46, 54, 64, 68, 90, 100, 108, 110, 114, 124, 132, 134, 142, 144, 155, 156
BGP 56
B-ISDN 102, 112
blocking mode 28
Border Gateway Protocol, see BGP
Border Intermediate System (BIS) 56
bridge ID 26
bridges .... 12, 20, 24, 64, ... 66, 68, 102, 154
configuration messages .... 26, ... 28, 34
designated 26
learning 20
loop prevention 24, 32, 34
performance 34
root 26, 28
SR 24, 30, 32, 34
SRT 24, 30, 36
SR-TB 24, 32
transparent 24, 30, 34
Broadband ISDN, see B-ISDN
burst mode 116, 118, 123

C
CCITT 10, 56
cell switching 110
cells 102, 110, 112, 114, 120
CIR 116
circuit switching 110
client/server computing .... 78, 94, ... 124, 148
CMIP 146
CMOL 148
CMOT 146
collapsed backbone .... 40, 46, ... 126, 134, 136
Common Transport Semantics 14
Common User Access 14
concentrators 134
confederation 56
configuration messages (bridges) 24
congestion 32, 34, 48, 50,

.......110, 112, 122, 123, 142, 144
connectionless service 10, 18,
....108, 120
connection-oriented 120
convergence 46, 62
conversion.......24, 36, 132, 142, 154
core 46, 52, 56, 68
Corporation for Open Systems
 (COS)..148
cost (bridges) 26
cost (routing)...................................60
Countdown Counter....................104
counting to infinity 48

D
data compression 66
Data Link Switching (DLS)........140
DCE 88, 152
DECnet 16, 132, 150, 152
designated bridge 26
directory service................18, 80, 82
disk mirroring 82
distance vector 48, 56, 60, 62
distributed backbone...................136
Distributed Computing Environ-
 ment, see DCE
Distributed Naming Service (DNS)
150
Distributed Queue Dual Bus,
 see DQDB
Distributed Relational Database Architecture (DRDA).................140
domain 50, 54, 60, 86
Domain Name Service (DNS) 18
dotted decimal notation................58
DQDB 102, 104, 118,
 ....120, 122, 123, 134
dual bus 105

E
EGP 56
End Node 14, 144

Ethernet.....................28, 36, 64, 82,
 86, 90, 100, 108, 124, 134, 136
Ethernet switch 38
Ethernet switching 114
EtherTalk 138
Exterior Gateway Protocol, see EGP

F
FDDI..........................90, 100, 108,
 ....114, 120, 134, 136
FDDI-II 120
forward bus 104
fragmentation......................106, 120
frame relay 102, 116, 123, 126
frames, definition..........................10

G
gateway 12, 20,102
global naming 80, 84, 152
GOSIP...................................58, 146

H
HELLO 50, 52, 60
High-Speed Serial Interface (HSSI)
102
holddown 48
hop count 46, 48, 60
host ID 58
hubs..................................12, 24,
 40, 68, 114, 126, 134, 136, 156
 switching............................38, 40

I
IDP...16
IETF................18, 56, 68, 122, 146
IGRP 48, 62
integrated bridge/routers........24, 40,
 ....68, 126
Integrated IS/IS.....................62, 68,
 ....146, 150, 152
integrated routing.........................62
inter-domain routing 54, 56
Inter-Domain Routing Protocol

INDEX

(IDRP) 56
Internet 18, 56, 68, 146, 150
Internet Activities Board (IAB) ... 18
Internet Engineering Task Force,
  see IETF
Internet Protocol, see IP
interoperability 120
intra-domain routing 54
IP 18, 36, 46, 58, 62, 64, 66,
  ..68, 84, 122, 142, 144, 146, 156
IPC 92
IPX 16, 62, 144
IPX Link State Routing Protocol
  (ILSR) 68
IS/IS 50, 52, 62, 68, 146
ISO 56
isochronous 20, 110, 120, 122
Isochronous Ethernet 114

L

LAN Manager 80, 86, 88
LAN Server 80, 88
LANtastic 80, 88
LAT 16, 64
link state 50, 60, 146
  directories 54
  flooding 50
  packets 52
  protocols 50
LLC 10, 36, 108
load sharing 34, 66
Local Area Transport, see LAT
local polling 36
LocalTalk 82, 100
Logical Link Control, see LLC
LSP, see link state
LU 6.2 .... 14, 92, 144

M

MAC 10, 108
MAN 100, 118, 120
Media Access Control, see MAC

Message Queue Manager (MQM)
  92
Metropolitan Area Networks,
  see MAN
middleware 12, 14, 36, 76,
  .... 92, 93, 94, 132, 144
migration 118, 126
MOP 64
MQM 144
multicast
  address 26, 66
  bit 30
  frames 30
multiprocessing 82, 86
  asymmetrical 86, 88
  symmetrical 86, 94
multi-protocol 94, 116, 132
multitasking 82

N

Named Pipes, see NP
neighbor 50, 52, 56
neighbor discovery 50
NetBIOS 14, 64, 66, 86
NetWare 16, 76, 80,
  .... 82, 84, 88, 94, 124, 150
NetWare Lite 82
NetWare Loadable Module (NLM)
  82
Network Control Program (NCP) 64
Network Entity Title (NET) 58
network ID 58
network management 114, 118,
  122, 124, 126, 136
Network Node 144
network operating system, see NOS
Network Service Access Points
  (NSAP) 58
NOS 6, 78, 80,
  .... 82, 84, 88, 94, 132, 150
NP 86, 92

NTS/2 88

O
OC-3 .... 102, 108, 114
Open Network Nodes (ONN) 144
Open Software Foundation (OSF)
.... 88, 152
OS/2 .... 86, 88, 90, 92
OS/400 14
OSF/1 152
OSI 10, 50, 52, 58, 62, 68, 76,
    ...84, 92, 132, 146, 148, 150, 152
OSPF 46, 50, 60, 62, 68, 142, 146

P
PA slots 104, 122, 123
packet switching 110
passthrough 36, 40
path discovery 30
Pathworks 150
payload 102, 106, 120
peer services 14, 86
performance 24, 38, 46, 66, 68,
    122, 123, 124, 132, 136, 142, 156
pipe 86
poll spoofing 36, 142
priority 110, 142, 144
private network 118
proxy polling 36

Q
QA slot 104

R
reachability 48
redistribution 60
repeaters 20, 138
Request Counter 104
reverse bus 104
RFC 18
RFC 1294 .... 116, 122
RIP 46, 48, 60, 62, 68, 146
risers 134

root ID 26
root port 26
route aging 32
route designators 30
route discovery 32
router backplane 46, 68, 126, 136
routers 12, 20,
    46, 48, 52, 60, 66, 68, 102, 114,
    120, 126, 132, 134, 136, 138, 150
    border 54
    designated 50
    dialup 66, 154
    external 54
    internal 54
    Level 1 54
    Level 2 .... 54, 56
    local 54
    loop prevention 60
routing information (RI) field 30, 34
routing protocol 46, 60, 62,
    .... 68, 146, 150
Routing Table Maintenance Protocol, see RTMP
RPC 92, 144, 150, 152
RTMP 62, 68

S
SDH 102, 108
SDLC 36, 40, 140, 142
server 12, 38, 76, 78, 82, 86,
    .... 88, 134, 136, 138, 150, 155
Ships in the Night, see SIN
SIP 108
skinny stack 148
slot 104
SMDS 102, 106, 118, 120,
    .... 122, 123, 126, 134
SNA 14, 16, 24, 36, 40, 64,
    66, 122, 132, 140, 142, 152, 156
    subarea routing 64, 140, 152
    timeouts 66, 142

INDEX

SNI..106
SNMP 94, 146
SONET 102, 108, 118, 126, 134
source routing, see bridges (SR)
spanning tree..24, 26, 28, 29, 34, 35
specifically routed frames.............30
split horizon 48
SPP..16
spread spectrum technology 154
SPX..16
SQL..92
StreetTalk......................................84
subnetworking 54
Switched Multimegabit Data Service, see SMDS
switching bridge 38, 39, 40
Synchronous Digital Hierarchy, see SDH
Synchronous Optical Network, see SONET
System 7 .... 76, 80
Systems Network Architecture, see SNA

T

T-1 ....40, 100, 102, 108,
..............110, 114, 120, 124, 126
TCP/IP 14, 16, 18, 36, 40,
....................62, 68, 86, 132, 140,
..............144, 146, 148, 150, 152
Telnet protocol......................18, 152
threads..152
timeouts (general).........................66
Token Ring ....
40, 82, 86, 88, 90, 91, 100, 106,
108, 124, 134, 136, 140, 142, 155
token ring 30, 36
topology maps..............................46
tower 150, 152
tower set......................................152

Transmission Control Protocol
(TCP) 18
transparent bridge, see bridges
transparent frame..........................30
tunnel.................. 24, 32, 36, 64, 132

U

UNIX............................... 18, 76, 80,
84, 86, 88, 90, 92, 94, 148, 152
unroutable traffic.......................... 64

V

VINES 76, 80, 84, 86, 88, 124
virtual circuit service............ 10, 18,
....104, 116

W

wide-area 32, 40,66,100, 106,
.... 110,116, 118, 124, 126, 144
Windows NT 88
wireless LANs..................... 12, 154

X

X Window interface 148
X.25.. 86
X.500.. 80
X/Open, see XTI
Xerox Network Systems, see XNS
XNS.. 14, 16
XTI 148, 152